"In this fine study of crucial s[...]
mind, and mission, Michael W. Pahl not only provides a sketch
of how Jesus read the Bible—thereby helping followers of Jesus
read the Bible—but also provides a template of the formative
teachings of Jesus. A splendid book in many ways."
—**SCOT MCKNIGHT**, author and teacher

"Hallelujah! Michael W. Pahl has the heart of a disciple, the
soul of a poet, and the mind of a scholar. His masterful mid-
rashim (or "fan fictions" as he calls them) are as vivid as they are
vibrant, and they will be appreciated both by those who have
just decided to follow Jesus and by developed disciples with
an eye for excellent exegesis. In these pages I entrust you to a
teacher who doesn't merely love the Scriptures but loves their
nonviolent-Messiah to whom they perfectly point."
—**JARROD MCKENNA**, Australian peace award–winning social
change educator, pastor at Steeple Church in Melbourne, and
cohost of the *InVerse Podcast*

"In this thoroughly engaging book, Michael W. Pahl invites
us to think more deeply about who Jesus was and is, what it
means to follow him, and why his message and mission continue to be good news for today's fractured and hurting world. *The
Word Fulfilled* reminds Christians, who are sometimes inclined
to distance Jesus from the Old Testament, that this good news
is deeply embedded in 'Jesus' Bible' and is a continuation of
God's purposes throughout the biblical story. Written in con-
versational prose, with imaginative stories that draw readers
into Jesus' first-century world, the book demonstrates a wealth
of New Testament scholarship in a way that is accessible for a
wide audience."
—**SHEILA KLASSEN-WIEBE**, associate professor of New
Testament at Canadian Mennonite University

"How did Jesus learn to read Scripture? And how did he teach his followers, ancient and modern, to do so? Combining careful scholarship, fictional vignettes, and insightful, challenging probes into the priorities of Jesus, Michael W. Pahl invites readers to join him in choosing the Jesus way."

—**TIMOTHY J. GEDDERT**, professor emeritus at Fresno Pacific Biblical Seminary and author of *The Beginning of the Story*

"Any reader of the New Testament will be aware of how Scripture is fulfilled in the ministry of Jesus, but in this accessible and lucid book, Michael W. Pahl helps us appreciate the fulfilled Word through the eyes of Jesus and the New Testament writers themselves. By understanding more fully how Jesus fulfilled Scripture in his day, we see more clearly how that is so for readers today."

—**PAUL N. ANDERSON**, professor of biblical and Quaker studies at George Fox University

THE
WORD
FULFILLED

THE WORD FULFILLED

READING THE BIBLE WITH JESUS

MICHAEL W. PAHL

Herald
PRESS

Harrisonburg, Virginia

Herald Press
PO Box 866, Harrisonburg, Virginia 22803
www.HeraldPress.com

Library of Congress Cataloging-in-Publication Data
Names: Pahl, Michael W., author.
Title: The word fulfilled : reading the Bible with Jesus / Michael W. Pahl.
Description: Harrisonburg, Virginia : Herald Press, [2024] | Includes
    bibliographical references.
Identifiers: LCCN 2024028914 (print) | LCCN 2024028915 (ebook) | ISBN
    9781513814483 (paperback) | ISBN 9781513814490 (hardcover) | ISBN
    9781513814506 (ebook)
Subjects: LCSH: Bible. Old Testament—Criticism, interpretation,
    etc.—History—Early church, ca. 30-600. | Christianity and other
    religions—Judaism. | BISAC: RELIGION / Biblical Criticism &
    Interpretation / Old Testament | RELIGION / Christianity / Mennonite
Classification: LCC BS1171.3 .P33 2024 (print) | LCC BS1171.3 (ebook) |
    DDC 221.606--dc23/eng/20240729
LC record available at https://lccn.loc.gov/2024028914
LC ebook record available at https://lccn.loc.gov/2024028915

Study guides are available for many Herald Press titles at www.HeraldPress.com.

THE WORD FULFILLED
© 2024 by Herald Press, Harrisonburg, Virginia 22803. 800-245-7894.
    All rights reserved.
Library of Congress Control Number: 2024028914
International Standard Book Number: 978-1-5138-1448-3 (paperback);
    978-1-5138-1449-0 (hardcover); 978-1-5138-1450-6 (ebook)

Design by Merrill Miller
Cover art adapted from xochicalco/Getty Images
Printed in United States of America

All scripture quotations, unless otherwise indicated, are taken from the New
Revised Standard Version Updated Edition. Copyright © 2021 National Council
of Churches of Christ in the United States of America. Used by permission. All
rights reserved worldwide.

28 27 26 25 24   10 9 8 7 6 5 4 3 2 1

Contents

To all those who, like me,
have heard the call of Jesus across the centuries, saying,
"Come, follow me."

Foreword

I MET MICHAEL W. PAHL when my husband and I worked at the same university with him. Michael was one of the New Testament professors, and my husband Shawn was one of the philosophy professors. I worked in student life.

Michael and his wife Larissa and their four children remain one of the most hospitable and loving families I have ever met. They regularly invited us and our gang of professors and their families over for dinner. We were like the Inklings—the discussion group at the University of Oxford that included the likes of C. S. Lewis and J. R. R. Tolkien. During our Inklings era, we shared many meals together as well as side-splitting laughter, tears, scholarship, stories, awe, and wonder. We all knew Michael to be a smart, gentle, gracious, funny scholar-pastor and secret Renaissance man. By "secret Renaissance man," I mean that he never boasted about himself, though he seemed to be good at nearly everything he put his hands to, including playing instruments. I never sat in on any of his classes, but I did, as it were, "sit in on" his life. So when Michael asked me to write this foreword, I happily obliged; I/we think the world of him and his family.

The Word Fulfilled is the fruit of one of the guiding questions of Michael's life: What Scriptures did Jesus read, and how did he understand them and himself? Michael seeks to understand how Jesus read and interpreted the Scriptures, that he might become more like Jesus in word and deed. As a New Testament scholar and pastor, Michael has the academic and experiential chops to write such a book, to put Jesus' world in context, to understand Scripture and the languages in which it was written, and to explain it to us so we can comprehend it. As a professor of spiritual formation, I often think about how Jesus was formed, how to become more like him, and how to guide my students in becoming more like Jesus in their attitudes, postures, and deeds so that when they speak about the good news, their lives back it up. I depend on scholar-pastors like Michael W. Pahl to help me teach and fulfill my calling in Christ's kingdom.

It is of utmost importance to know how Jesus interpreted and applied the Scriptures with which he was familiar. Jesus' interpretation and application are the quintessential guide for us, teaching us to love God and, to paraphrase Michael, *to love God by loving our neighbors.* Two of the concepts in these pages that really drove me into contemplation are those of Jubilee and God's desire for "mercy not sacrifice." I will not go into great detail—for that, you have to read this excellent book. But Michael's fresh explanation of these concepts and those found in the other chapters fuel my faith. His words motivate me to become more like Jesus by examining myself and to continue helping the church in the United States become more like Christ.

Something to know about Michael as you read his words is that he practices what he preaches. When we lived in community with him, we witnessed many things, including his attitude and posture toward power-hungry Christians at the university who, in street slang, did him dirty. My husband and I, and others, were beyond furious. We defended him. Cried for him and his family. And wondered how those who profess to know Jesus and the Scriptures could act like the devil's henchmen to someone so upright. He went through, as it were, a Job experience. Self-righteous, cruel, ignorant, deceitful, Christian people acted like Joseph's brothers who threw him into the pit and then sold him off to enslavers. And because we and others defended our colleague, because we functioned as whistle-blowers about systemic lies, deceit, and injustice, they did the same to us. None of us regret it one bit, even though it cost all of us our jobs.

Through it all, Michael concretely loved his neighbors who functioned as enemies. When he talks about the abuse of power and oppressive people and loving God by loving others, he knows of what he speaks. It took me ten years to forgive the institution and its people, that behind-the-scenes toxic system, for what it did to Michael, his family, and others. It was bad. Really bad. Evil. However, Michael did not respond in kind. He and his family (and others) were crushed. And yet I am here to tell you that I have witnessed resurrection power. In 1 Corinthians 11:1, the apostle Paul exhorts the Corinthian church to imitate him even as he imitates Christ. I think of Michael similarly. When I imitate Michael W. Pahl in how he loves God through loving his neighbors and enemies, I imitate Christ.

This book is worth more than its weight in gold. Would that many, many Christians read it and put it into practice to become like Jesus.

—Marlena Graves
Author and assistant professor of spiritual formation at the School of Theological Studies and Northeastern Seminary on the campus of Roberts Wesleyan University

Preface

THE SEEDS FOR THIS BOOK were planted in a sermon series I preached while serving as pastor at Morden Mennonite Church in Morden, Manitoba. These seeds took root and grew in a subsequent continuing education course I taught through Canadian Mennonite University. I am grateful to both the good folks of Morden Mennonite and the excellent university that is CMU for both opportunities.

I have long had an interest in what scholars call "the New Testament use of the Old Testament." What were the Scriptures the New Testament authors had available to them? What texts from these Scriptures did they especially like to refer to? Which texts especially shaped their thinking about God and God's work in the world? How did they read these texts?

It occurred to me at some point that, particularly as an Anabaptist-Mennonite striving to walk in the way of Jesus, it would be good for me to focus these questions on Jesus himself.[1] As those who seek to follow Jesus, disciples of Jesus striving to learn and live the way of Jesus, we would do well to learn how Jesus read his Scriptures so that we can read our Scriptures in the way he did.

And thus the seeds were planted in a sermon series, they grew into a continuing education course, and now they flower in the form of this book. The fruit will be in the actual difference these ideas make in the lives of readers like you. Thank you for taking up and reading this book to learn along with me.

Many others also deserve thanks for seeing this book through to publication.

I'm grateful to Herald Press for contacting me about writing a new book. It has been thirteen years since my last authored book, and for much of that time I had no inclination to write another one. It was an email from Amy Gingerich, itself prodded by my friend Marlena Graves, which prompted me to reconsider. Thanks to Marlena for contacting Amy, and to Amy for reaching out to me. Thanks also to Laura Leonard Clemens, Sara Versluis, Elisabeth Ivey, Ardell Stauffer, and the rest of the team at Herald Press for carrying the work through to completion. You have been terrific to work with, and you have unquestionably made this a better book.

My day job has gone back and forth between academics and church ministry over the years, and currently I am serving as executive minister for Mennonite Church Manitoba. I am grateful to the MCM board for granting me some study leave time to complete the manuscript and then later to do the necessary editing. I'm grateful also to the CMU Library, especially Wes Bergen, for their assistance in providing me with the resources I needed to complete my research for this project.

How do you say thank you to those who walk with you day by day, making your life possible? There aren't words to express how grateful I am for my family. Milly, Molly, and Mandy, in your mix of comfort, cuteness, and annoyance you give us lots of smiles and laughter (to clarify: these are our dogs and cat). Amelia and Séverine, Mia, Matthew, and Adalynne, you give us so much joy, and I love how the tables have turned for us, where now we are learning so much from you. Thank you for being who you are, for the ways you contribute to this beautiful, joyful mess of a mutual support society that is our family. Larissa, I am glad every day for that infamous poke in the back that led to our life together. Thank you for your companionship, your inspiration, your patience, your faithful presence, and your sweet, sweet love.

✳ ✳ ✳

A few notes on the text that follows.

Formal scripture quotations, with full citation, are from the New Revised Standard Version Updated Edition. Less formal ones reflect my own translation or adaptation.

As this is not a work intended for scholars, I have kept notes to a minimum, using them primarily to reference direct quotations of or strong allusions to another author's work. Sources for the historical claims made throughout the book can be found in the "Digging Deeper" section at the back.

That "Digging Deeper" section provides some historical and cultural background for the ideas and stories reflected in the rest of the book. Some readers may opt to start there, to have that background in mind while reading the book. There is also a study guide at the end of the book which can assist in using the book for individual or small group study.

It feels like this shouldn't need to be said, but God does not have gender. As I've said in teaching about this, being intentionally provocative, "God is not a woman. Neither is she a man."

I've tried, therefore, to avoid masculine and feminine pronouns for God, instead preferring to follow Rabbi Danya Ruttenberg's oft-repeated advice in her writing and social media posts: "The pronoun for God is God."[2]

I would like to get away from all gendered language related to God, but I've struggled to find non-gendered language that adequately expresses what I want to say for a few word groups. In a book that attempts to describe how first-century Jews thought about their Scriptures and about God, I also feel some compulsion to reflect the language of first-century Judaism related to God.

One of these word groups is the language of "lord" in reference to God or to Jesus.

I have followed the practice of many modern English translations, including the NRSV, in using LORD (small capitals) for the divine name—although I've done this not only in translation of the Hebrew Bible but also in my depictions of first-century Jews speaking of God. This is simply convention; the divine name doesn't mean "lord." Rather, it reflects the Hebrew for "I am." This use of LORD came about because, in oral reading of the Hebrew Bible, Jews have read "Adonai" when coming across the divine name, and Adonai means "Lord." They do this in obedience to the third commandment —"You shall not make wrongful use of the name of the LORD your God" (Exodus 20:7)—since they view the divine name as holy.

Since LORD is already understood to represent the divine name, it seems the simplest way to convey that the revealed name of God is being referenced. YHWH or Yahweh is often used, but many Christians avoid these out of respect for the Jewish faith. I follow their lead throughout the book, especially since I'm describing how first-century Jews spoke of God. Further, the use of "Lord" instead of "LORD" for the divine name doesn't work: in most of the New Testament writings, "Lord" (Greek *kurios*) refers to Jesus, not to "God the Father," the God of Israel as revealed to Moses.

This language of "Lord" for Jesus is tricky, however. In any given New Testament text where "Lord" (*kurios*) is used for Jesus, one or more of at least four possible allusions are at play: (1) the use of Adonai for the divine name in oral reading of the Hebrew Bible (*kurios*, "lord," in the Old Greek translation); (2) the use of "lord" as "master" for rabbis in early Judaism; (3) the use of "lord" for household patriarchs, masters of their household in the patriarchal world of the first century; and (4) the use of "lord" in reference to Caesar, the Roman emperor, as ultimate master over the wider "household" that was the Roman Empire. I have kept the language of "lord" in reference to Jesus where one or more of these echoes seem to be in the air—which is pretty much all the time.

The language of "king" and "kingdom" in reference to God or Jesus is also tricky.

"Kindom" is a popular choice, but it loses, or at least dulls, the explicit political resonance of the Hebrew and Greek words. It can also make people think that God's reign is about biological kin, which is not at all the case. I like "reign," or even "dominion," as alternatives, and I try to use them where possible. However, I'm acutely aware that the phrases "kingdom of God" and "kingdom of heaven" have centuries of Christian use behind them and thus signal "This is what Jesus talked about!" in a way that "reign of God" or "God's dominion" do not.

I have avoided "king" in reference to God but have kept "king" in reference to Jesus when it has seemed necessary.

Similar dynamics are at play in whether to use "son of man" or "human being" (or even "humanity").

The basic question I'm asking in this book is a simple one: How did Jesus read his Bible, and what does that mean for how we as Jesus-followers should read ours? While the question might be simple, answering it is not easy, however, due to gaps in our historical knowledge. Some historically-informed imagination is therefore needed. Readers will see this imagination throughout the book—and even a bit of whimsy.

In each chapter, I have written a short vignette, a fictional episode from the early life of Jesus, to situate the ideas being described in Jesus' first-century context. The temptation in fictionalizing episodes of Jesus' life is to use Aramaicized names and terms for people and things to give the story a greater verisimilitude—for example, to use "Yeshua" instead of "Jesus." After all, Aramaic was the mother language spoken by Jesus and his Galilean contemporaries. However, I've mostly resisted that temptation. You, dear reader, will discover those times when the temptation has proven irresistible.

Preparing to Read the Bible with Jesus

HOW SHOULD WE read the Bible?

For many Christians, this isn't even a question. They simply pick up their Bible and read it. It makes sense to them, and they act on what they understand it to mean. "The Bible says it, I believe it, that settles it," as the saying goes.

However, many of us are discovering that this isn't as simple as we once thought.

The small town I grew up in had several churches—typical of small towns on the Canadian prairies, especially in rural Alberta. United Church, Anglican, Roman Catholic, Baptist, Mennonite (two types), Christian Reformed (two churches), Latter-day Saints, a nondenominational church or two—all of them read the same Bible, but very differently.

There are thousands of Christian denominations worldwide. Many of these were formed because their founders read the Bible differently than the churches they left. Each of them was convinced they were reading the "clear meaning of the Bible." The result, though, is many different interpretations of the Bible and Christian faith, some of which are directly at odds with one another.

Clearly, the Bible's meaning isn't as clear as we like to think.

Here's another angle on this problem of "pervasive interpretive pluralism,"[1] as sociologist of religion Christian Smith calls it: there have been many times when Christians or churches have been convinced they have read the Bible correctly, only to change their minds later.

For example, through most of church history, Christians almost universally held that slavery was an acceptable, even God-ordained, institution. For the educated elite, this was grounded in their reading of the Bible. Today, this is considered a fringe belief. (In contemporary contexts, it has typically been found only among extremist groups, but it is experiencing a troubling resurgence among Christian nationalists.) Other examples are not hard to come by—flat earth, young earth, an earth-centered universe—all these and more were once vigorously defended by appealing to the clear meaning of Scripture. Now they are relegated to the margins of mainstream Christian belief.

Again, it's clear that the Bible's meaning isn't as clear as we like to think.

This problem has had a considerable impact, especially in North America and Europe. Even in these secular, liberal democracies, religious undercurrents are strong, often fueled by how various groups read their scriptures (the Bible most prominently, as Christianity remains the most represented religion in these regions). These religious undercurrents can profoundly influence politics, and therefore all of society. Indeed, in some instances these are not "undercurrents" but waves of religious zeal that are crashing violently on the shores of Western democracies.

So the question of how we as Christians should read the Bible isn't as straightforward, or as benign, as we might be tempted to think.

This book isn't going to solve this problem. It does, though, make an appeal to read the Bible in a particular way. Here's my audacious claim: *Jesus read his Scriptures in a distinctive way, and so we should follow Jesus in the way he read his Scriptures.*

The New Testament uses a variety of terms and ideas to emphasize the importance of following Jesus.

"Follow me" is Jesus' invitation to the Galilean fishermen who became his first disciples (Mark 1:17). He repeats this call throughout the Gospels as he invites people to join him as his disciples (Matthew 8:22; Mark 2:14; 8:34; 10:21; John 1:43; 21:19).

This language of "disciple" itself implies a following. As we'll discover, the disciples of a first-century rabbi were expected not only to learn their rabbi's teachings but also to imitate their rabbi's way of life. If the rabbi were an itinerant teacher, like Jesus, that could mean literally following the rabbi as they moved from place to place.

In Luke's story of the early church in Acts, the early Christians describe themselves as members of "the Way," suggesting that they saw their life of faith as a path to walk, a way of salvation marked out for us by Jesus (Acts 9:2; 18:25; 19:23).

Paul highlights the goal of the Christian life as being formed in the image of Christ (Romans 8:28–29; 2 Corinthians 3:18), and the life of faith as an "imitation of Christ": "Be imitators of me, as I am of Christ," he says to the Corinthian believers (1 Corinthians 11:1).

Hebrews urges its readers to "run with perseverance the race that is set before us, looking to Jesus, the pioneer and perfecter of faith" (12:1–2).

First Peter declares that Jesus has left us an example of suffering, "so that [we] should follow in his steps" (2:21).

First John bluntly sums this all up: "Whoever says, 'I abide in him,' ought to walk in the same way as he walked" (2:6).

Viewing the Christian life as following Jesus has been a particular focus of Anabaptist understandings of Christianity, including the stream of Christianity in which I've chosen to swim, the Mennonites. Early Anabaptist Hans Denck, living five hundred years ago, held this as his motto: "No one may truly know Christ except one who follows him in life."[2]

As Christians, we seek to follow Jesus not only in learning, meditating on, and obeying his teachings. We also do so by observing and imitating his way of life. And an important facet of both Jesus' teachings and his way of life was his use of his Scriptures—the Jewish Scriptures, the Hebrew Bible, or what Christians know as the Old Testament.

It makes sense, therefore, that if we want to follow Jesus in his teachings and his way of life, that should extend to learning about and emulating the way he read his Scriptures.

Over the next seven chapters, we are going to spend some time with Jesus. We're going to observe how he read his Scriptures and explore what this might mean for how we as Christians should read our Scriptures.

We're going to read the Bible with Jesus.

For this experiment in experiential learning, I've chosen seven of the most prominent Old Testament passages quoted by Jesus in the Gospels. These seven passages are not simply the ones that Jesus refers to most often, though they are certainly at or near the top of that list. These seven passages are noteworthy for their significance for the gospel authors and, it would seem, for Jesus himself.

An early Jewish "creed," the Shema:

Hear, O Israel: The LORD is our God, the LORD alone. You shall love the LORD your God with all your heart and with all your soul and with all your might. Keep these words that I am commanding you today in your heart. Recite them to your children and talk about them when you are at home and when you are away, when you lie down and when you rise. Bind them as a sign on your hand, fix them as an emblem on your forehead, and write them on the doorposts of your house and on your gates. (Deuteronomy 6:4–9)

A summary commandment from God:

You shall love your neighbor as yourself: I am the LORD. (Leviticus 19:18)

The mission of God's servant:

The spirit of the Lord GOD is upon me
　　because the LORD has anointed me;
he has sent me to bring good news to the oppressed,
　　to bind up the brokenhearted,
to proclaim liberty to the captives
　　and release to the prisoners,

to proclaim the year of the LORD's favor . . .
(Isaiah 61:1–2)

The call of God's prophet:
Go and say to this people:
"Keep listening, but do not comprehend;
keep looking, but do not understand."
Make the mind of this people dull,
and stop their ears,
and shut their eyes,
so that they may not look with their eyes
and listen with their ears
and comprehend with their minds
and turn and be healed. (Isaiah 6:9–10)

A prophetic rebuke:
For I desire steadfast love and not sacrifice,
the knowledge of God rather than burnt offerings.
(Hosea 6:6)

A promise of God's victory to the Messiah, the Son of God:
The LORD says to my lord,
"Sit at my right hand
until I make your enemies your footstool."
(Psalm 110:1)

And a vision of God's dominion given to a Son of Man:
As I watched in the night visions,
I saw one like a human being
coming with the clouds of heaven.
And he came to the Ancient One

and was presented before him.
To him was given dominion
and glory and kingship,
that all peoples, nations, and languages
should serve him.
His dominion is an everlasting dominion
that shall not pass away,
and his kingship is one
that shall never be destroyed. (Daniel 7:13–14)

Let's begin, then, reading the Bible with Jesus.

ONE

The Shema

Hear, O Israel: The LORD is our God, the LORD alone. You shall love the LORD your God with all your heart and with all your soul and with all your might. Keep these words that I am commanding you today in your heart. Recite them to your children and talk about them when you are at home and when you are away, when you lie down and when you rise. Bind them as a sign on your hand, fix them as an emblem on your forehead, and write them on the doorposts of your house and on your gates.

—DEUTERONOMY 6:4–9

MY HOLY BIBLE

One of my most sacred possessions is an old NIV Student Bible. Black hardcover, held together by packing tape, cushioned in a black zippered Bible cover with thin green and purple trim.

It's the Bible I received from my home church in Coaldale, Alberta, after graduating from high school. It was my Bible when I left that church and began participating in a small but vibrant Baptist church plant, where I was baptized. It was my Bible when I then went through a crisis of faith, searching for faith in other traditions and religions, searching for reasons for faith at all.

It was my Bible when I experienced what I call my "grace awakening," when God's Spirit stirred in my heart and I picked up this Bible and read through it in massive doses: Genesis through Deuteronomy in one day, all of Psalms the next, Isaiah in a single afternoon, the gospel accounts one after the other, all Paul's letters in an evening. It was my Bible through college and seminary and back into college again, when I began my career of teaching the Bible. It was my Bible when my wife and I got married, when each of our children was born—all these events are listed inside its front cover.

Eventually, this Bible got worn out and I had to set it aside. I had also outgrown it. The notes I had written in the margins, when I was so convinced I had the clear meaning of this or that verse—I now alternate between smiling and cringing when I read them. Sometimes my past self was surprisingly insightful. Other times my past self was badly wrong.

Regardless, this Bible is still one of my most sacred possessions. That's not because of all those notes in the margins, all the color-coded highlighting. It's not even because it's a Bible and it has some special status simply because it's a Bible. No, it is one of my most sacred possessions because through this Bible, God brought me to Jesus, my Savior and my Lord.

Through this Bible I met Jesus, and my life has never been the same since.

The Bible is important to us as Christians. Second Timothy 3:15 says that our "sacred writings" are "able to instruct [us] for salvation through faith in Christ Jesus." That's their primary purpose: through the Bible we meet Jesus, our Savior and our Lord. These scriptures are "inspired by God"—or better, "breathed into by God"—2 Timothy 3:16 goes on to say, which makes them "useful" to us: "useful for teaching, for reproof, for correction, and for training in righteousness," training in the way of Jesus.

The Bible is important to us as Christians. This has always been so. But how does the Bible actually *work*? How does it "instruct" us for salvation in Jesus? How does it become "useful" for training us in the way of Jesus?

How should we read the Bible?

As we explored in the opening chapter, there is good reason for Christians to answer this question by looking to Jesus, to see how he read his Bible, and then to follow him in this.

So how did Jesus read his Bible?

But as soon as we ask *this* question, we encounter a problem: Jesus didn't *have* a Bible, at least nothing like my NIV Student Bible.

JESUS' "BIBLE"

We often take our Bibles for granted. I probably have two dozen different printed Bibles: a couple of Hebrew Bibles, some Greek New Testaments, Bibles in other languages, many different English versions. If we need a Bible, we just go to a bookstore and pick one up—or more likely, we simply download a Bible app or look it up online.[1]

And so we take reading our Bibles for granted. We encourage personal Bible reading. We encourage small group Bible study. We believe this is something important for our Christian life. We assume it's the way Christians have always done things.

But, as good as this can be—my own story is testimony to this—this "personal Bible reading" is a recent innovation. It's a perk of modern Western Christianity. The idea that I can have my own Bible—all the biblical writings collected into a single book—and I can read it on my own in my own language is something most Christians through history and around the world couldn't even have imagined doing, let alone been able to do.

I'd love to walk through the whole history of the Bible and how it got from a first manuscript written in proto-Hebrew in ancient Israel all the way to my well-worn NIV Student Bible. It's a fascinating story, but it would take another book to sketch it out.

Instead, let's take a step back into the synagogue of a small Jewish village in the hills of Galilee two thousand years ago and check out the Bible as Jesus would have known it. Because that's where Jesus' "Bible"—his written Scriptures—would have been: the village synagogue.

There's a lot we don't know about synagogues in the first century, but we know some things. Synagogues at the time of Jesus were likely community centers as much as they were religious centers—which makes sense when an entire village is Jewish and community and religious life is all one common life. It's likely, too, that most small-village synagogues were fairly simple affairs, not like the few stone structures whose remains have survived to this day.

The synagogue in Nazareth—we'll imagine it as a humble mud-brick structure attached to the home of a synagogue elder—would have had at most a few biblical scrolls. These may not have even been housed in the synagogue itself. They could have been kept by an elder or a wealthy patron, brought out for reading and study at most a few times a week, most importantly on the Sabbath.

The first and most essential of these scrolls was a large one, or maybe five smaller ones kept together: the Torah, the five books of Moses. This includes Genesis, Exodus, Leviticus, Numbers, and Deuteronomy. Another likely scroll would have been the Psalms—their hymnbook, you might say, but likely with only one copy for the whole congregation. They probably also had a scroll of Isaiah, maybe a scroll of Jeremiah, perhaps a scroll of "the Twelve" (what we call the Minor Prophets), but not likely many more.

These scrolls—the Torah, the Psalms, and some of the Prophets—would all have been handwritten, carefully transcribed by professional scribes. The Torah scroll might have been made of animal skin, the others probably from the papyrus plant. These scrolls would have been very expensive—which is why almost no private individuals owned them. That, and the fact that they were likely written in Hebrew, which was not the everyday language of people in Galilee.

This, then, was Jesus' "Bible": a small collection of separate scrolls including the Law of Moses, some of the Prophets, and some of the Writings—not even all of what Christians call the Old Testament—written in an ancient language that people didn't speak most of the time, the only village copy held in the local synagogue and brought out for reading once or twice a week.

So if we have an image in our head of Jesus having his personal devotions, sitting with his Bible and reading it prayerfully—well, that's just not the way it was. Jesus had no Bible like we do. This kind of book that we call a Bible—these specific writings, all bound together in a single book, accessible and readable by individual, average people—was still many centuries away from reality.

But clearly the Scriptures were important to Jesus, as they were to all Jews of his time. If Jesus couldn't literally "read his Bible," how did he engage the writings Jews considered Scripture? A few ways, probably.

Jesus would have heard the Scriptures read and sung in the synagogue every Sabbath. Every Saturday, the village would gather together to pray some prayers, sing some psalms, hear a passage read from the Torah and another from the Prophets, and have an elder or honored guest teach on these passages.

Jesus could well have gone to synagogue school as a young Jewish boy. This is far from certain, especially in a small village like Nazareth. But if he did go to synagogue school, from the age of five or six he would have spent part of each day learning from a local elder or a visiting rabbi: learning Hebrew so he could read the scrolls on the Sabbath, memorizing specific scripture passages orally by rote repetition, and as he got older, learning the different traditional interpretations of these passages.

But just as importantly, *Jesus would have heard specific scriptures sung or recited throughout the day,* in the home and out in the fields, all throughout his childhood, and he would have joined in with this as he grew up among his kin in Nazareth. The most important of these scriptures was the Shema.

EVENING AND MORNING

Jesus lay still on his woven bedroll, eyes closed as he listened to his parents praying the Shema outside. He slowly opened his eyes to see the early morning sun peeking through the doorway, dust glimmering in its rays.

He must have been sleeping for a long time, for that was also the last thing he remembered from the night before: Mary and Joseph reciting the central confession of their faith. "Hear, O Israel: The LORD is our God, the LORD alone. You shall love the LORD your God with all your heart, and with all your soul, and with all your might."

Granted, it had been a busy day the day before. He needed the sleep.

They had been at a wedding in another village a half day's walk away: Jesus' aunt had gotten married in Magdala. The wedding celebration was an elaborate affair, with several days of eating, drinking, singing, and dancing—and catching up on the family gossip. Yesterday morning had been filled with cleaning and packing before they had departed for home.

Jesus, like all the youngest children, had few responsibilities on a day like that. So they had spent the morning roaming the safest of the lower caves near the village, replaying stories of ancient valor. Most of his cousins were older than he was; he had to play Caleb to their Joshua, Jonathan to their David, Simon to their Judas Maccabee.

As he lay on his mat, listening to his parents chant the treasured words of the Shema, he smiled. Maybe someday, he thought, I can be like my namesake Joshua. Maybe I can even be David.

With this spark of an idea flickering in his soul, he sat up and joined in the Shema's final phrases: "I am the LORD your God who brought you out of the land of Egypt to be your God. I am the LORD your God."

THE SHEMA

This was Jesus' daily reality, all throughout his life, just as it was the reality of every devout Jew in Galilee: reciting the Shema, which began with Deuteronomy 6:4–9, twice every day. As the text itself says, "when you lie down and when you rise."

It's no surprise to anyone, therefore, that when the adult Jesus is asked what "the first and greatest commandment of the Law" is, he replies with the Shema (see Matthew 22:34–40; Mark 12:28–31). That's what everyone would expect, because that's what every Jew grew up confessing every single day, evening and morning.

Shema, Yisrael! Hear, O Israel!

Pay attention, everyone! This is important!

The LORD is our God, the LORD alone!

"The LORD" here is the holy name of God revealed to Moses as described in Exodus 3:13–15: God is the "I Am," the "One Who Is." In obedience to the third commandment (Exodus 20:7), Jews do not say the divine name. Instead, they replace it with "Adonai" in their scripture reading, which means "Lord." In many modern English versions, this is rendered with small capitals as LORD. (As noted earlier, you'll also see this throughout this book—no, God is not literally a "lord"!)

The LORD, the God who simply is, the one from whom and for whom all things exist, the one in whom we live and move and have our being, is the only true God there is. We make gods out of all kinds of things, many of them which start out as good things. Our idols are not just wood and stone, but also money and power and technology and sex and violence and political ideologies and social structures and more. The apostle Paul says in 1 Corinthians 8:5–6 that there are many such "gods and lords" in our world, but for Christians, there is only one true God, our Creator, and one true Lord, Jesus Christ, from whom and through whom all things exist.

> You shall love the LORD your God with all your heart, and with all your soul, and with all your might.

We are to love God with every dimension of our being: heart, soul, mind, strength. That is, we are to be devoted to God with everything that we are and do. We are to honor God in everything we think and say. We are to trust in God for everything that we need. All things owe their existence—and therefore their allegiance—to God. All of us, every one of us, and all of creation, in all its dimensions, is from God, and all exists for God's purposes.

The Shema, then, Jesus' "first and greatest commandment," is about undivided devotion to our Creator. And in Jesus' day, no one would have disputed that this is our highest calling.

THE SHEMA IN SEARCH OF AN ENDING

But this leads to a question: What exactly does this undivided devotion to God look like? How, practically speaking, do we show our love for God?

I wonder—how do you show your love for God in your everyday life? What behaviors or practices would you name as demonstrating that you are devoted to God in every aspect of your being?

In Jesus' day, there were many different ideas of what this undivided devotion to God could look like, what it means to "love God." I suspect these have parallels among us still today.

For all Jews in Jesus' day, loving God meant worshiping God, praising and thanking God for who God is and what God does, both in private and together, in synagogue and in the Jerusalem temple. Christians might think the same today: we show our undivided devotion to God by worshiping, praising, and thanking God, daily on our own, weekly in church.

For many Jews in Jesus' day, loving God meant being devoted to the Torah, studying and following the Law of Moses down to the letter. Many Christians think the same today: we show our undivided devotion to God by reading the Bible and seeking to be "biblical" in all we do.

For most Jews in Jesus' day, loving God meant being devoted to "purity," keeping sharp distinctions between "clean" and "unclean": avoiding "unclean" foods, "profane" behaviors, and "impure" people. Many think the same today: we show our undivided devotion to God by separating ourselves from all that is sinful, unrighteous, "impure."

For some Jews in Jesus' day, loving God meant being devoted to Israel, expelling the godless Romans, and making Israel great again. Some Christians think the same today: Christians show undivided devotion to God by trying to create and maintain a "Christian nation."

For a few Jews in Jesus' day, this love for God meant that people could well get hurt along the way; some were even willing to commit lethal violence to show their love for God. In fact, this was the apostle Paul before he met Jesus on the

Damascus road (Galatians 1:13–14), and some think the same today: we show our undivided devotion to God no matter how much it might hurt others, no matter how much harm it causes along the way.

All these ways of loving God still find approval among some of God's people. Some of these ways of loving God are even good and necessary. But none of these is how Jesus described the primary way we are to love God with all our heart, soul, mind, and strength.

For Jesus, the Shema could not simply stand on its own. We have proven throughout history that we can do a lot of terrible things to one another out of undivided devotion to God. Christians have shown their undivided devotion to God by arming themselves for crusades against Muslim "infidels." They've shown it by burning "heretics" at the stake, colonizing Indigenous lands and peoples, and enslaving African peoples deemed subhuman.

Yes, we've proven we can justify a lot of horrible behaviors by claiming we are simply "loving God."

So Jesus provided a second command that he said is "like the first," and together these are "the greatest commands" of God that sum up all the Law and the Prophets (see Matthew 22:37–40). Together these are humanity's highest calling.

We'll explore this "extended edition" of the Shema shortly, but here's a spoiler.

We don't love God by forcing others to live the way we believe God wants us to live.

We don't love God by creating a "Christian nation" that professes the right things and follows the right rituals and passes the right laws.

We don't love God by separating ourselves from impurity and sinners.

We don't even love God first and foremost by studying our Bibles or praising God, as good as those things are.

We love God by loving others.

TWO

The Shema, Extended Edition

You shall love your neighbor as yourself:
I am the LORD.

—LEVITICUS 19:18

TORAH DEBATE

Jesus walked into the village synagogue with a feeling that might be called "curious but nervous." He was six years old, growing in wisdom and in stature, in favor with God and others, and the synagogue elders had determined that the boys of Nazareth should have some formal education starting at age six.

So here Jesus was, curious but nervous as he took this important step into the open, sunlit room.

His best friend Judas nudged his elbow. "It's Rabbi Eleazar from Sepphoris," he whispered in awe, and then grabbed Jesus by the arm, stopping them both. "Look! I can't believe he's allowing Jonathan to be his disciple! My father says Jonathan's nothing but trouble!"

Jesus looked to where his friend was staring. In one corner of the room, an elderly man sat on the wooden bench against the wall, a group of youths sitting on the floor before him.

The old rabbi was awe-inspiring, but not in the way he dressed or in the way he spoke. Actually, his clothing was rather drab—a simple dun-colored cloak over a lighter, thinner tunic, plain tassels on the corners of his clothing, and ordinary sandals on his feet—and he had said nothing at all since they came into the synagogue.

Rather, it was something about Rabbi Eleazar's bearing, the way he looked at each of the young men before him through those soulful, twinkling eyes framed by a head and beard gone grey.

And there was trouble-making Jonathan: fifteen years old and utterly sure of himself, holding forth among the half-dozen disciples gathered from Sepphoris and the surrounding hill country.

"Rabbi Shammai refused even to honor the Gentile's demand," Jonathan was saying, voice raised in proper indignation. "Teach him the entire Torah while he stood on one foot, indeed! The very thought, that the whole Law of Moses could be summarized in just a few words!"

Heads nodded in agreement around him. These teenagers had already spent some years studying the Torah and its interpretations, and they knew there was still more study ahead of them.

Jesus stepped closer, into a shaft of sunlight, curious what Rabbi Eleazar might say in response.

"Ah, but you do not yet know the rest of the story," the venerable teacher said softly. All eyes turned to him. "Yes, it is true. The esteemed Rabbi Shammai cast out the Gentile seeker, insulted by his demand. But this Gentile, also a child of our Creator, went then to Rabbi Hillel. And do you know what Master Hillel said to this Gentile?"

The boys shook their heads as one.

"He accepted the man's challenge." The boys' eyes widened. Jesus leaned in still further.

"Yes, in truth, he did—I was there when it happened!" the old rabbi continued. "And while this Gentile seeker stood on one foot, Rabbi Hillel said to him these words: 'That which is hateful to you, do not do to your neighbor. That is the whole Torah; the rest is commentary. Go and learn.'"

As the rabbi's disciples began to repeat this teaching, committing it to memory, Jesus closed his eyes, letting the sunlight from the open window warm his face. Yes, he said to himself, something moving deep within his spirit. "Love your neighbor as yourself," as the Torah reading last Sabbath had said.

God's Law summed up in a single word: love.

COMMANDMENTS HEAVY AND LIGHT

As we've seen, Jesus didn't have a Bible, not like we do. He didn't have a bound collection of all the sacred writings we do, written in his everyday language and readable on his own. People didn't own Bibles of any kind. Rather, their written Scriptures were a few hand-copied scrolls of Torah and Prophets and Writings, stored in the synagogue and brought out for public reading a few times a week, especially on the Sabbath.

Even though Jesus didn't have a personal Bible, he still learned and engaged his Scriptures—but mostly aurally and orally: by ear and by mouth. By hearing and reciting the Shema, the call for Israel to love God with undivided devotion, each evening and morning. Or as in my story of Jesus at the synagogue, by learning the Torah as a child through rote memorization, and then as a youth learning about the traditions of the rabbis in interpreting the Torah.

The story I've told is made up, of course. I couldn't tell you whether Jesus had a childhood friend named Judas—though it's certainly plausible, given how common a name it was at the time. And we don't know for sure how or when—or even if—young Jewish boys in Galilee at that time studied the Torah and the traditions of the rabbis, especially in a small village synagogue. What I've described, however, is a possibility.

But the story the old Rabbi Eleazar told—the story about the two rabbis and the Gentile, non-Jewish seeker—is a traditional story about two real-life rabbis a generation older than Jesus.[1] And it fits with a question that many rabbis of that era spent a good bit of time discussing and debating: Which commandments in the Torah are "heavier" and which are "lighter"? That is, which commandments in the Law of Moses are most important?

THE GREATEST COMMANDMENT

Given all this, it would not have been odd for the adult Jesus to be confronted with this question: "Teacher, which commandment in the Law is the greatest?"

Jesus' response? "'You shall love the Lord your God with all your heart and with all your soul and with all your mind.' This is the greatest and first commandment. And a second is like it: 'You shall love your neighbor as yourself.' On these two commandments hang all the Law and the Prophets" (Matthew 22:37–40).

Jesus declaring "Love the LORD your God" to be the greatest commandment would also have been entirely unsurprising, as we've seen. That was the opening of the Shema, after all, recited twice a day by every devout Jew. Naturally it's the greatest commandment.

It's also not surprising that Jesus emphasizes "Love your neighbor as yourself." Leviticus 19, where this commandment is from, has often been seen by Jewish interpreters as a commentary on the Ten Commandments, and some form of "love your neighbor as yourself" was highlighted by several teachers and sages from that time—including the famous Rabbi Hillel.

It's not even surprising that Jesus brings both the "vertical" (obligations toward God) and the "horizontal" (obligations toward others) together as a way of describing the Law of Moses. The notion that the Law in general, and the Ten Commandments specifically, describe both vertical and horizontal obligations has been a common one among Jews through history.

But here Jesus goes in a distinctive direction: he takes the specific "love of neighbor" commandment of Leviticus 19:18

and attaches it to the specific "love of God" commandment of the Shema in Deuteronomy 6:4–9, and he holds these two together in a way that makes love of neighbor a description of *how* we love God. The second commandment is "like" (Greek *homoios*) the first, Jesus says in Matthew's gospel: love of neighbor is "of a similar nature to," even "as important as," love of God.

In other words, according to Jesus, we love God, first and foremost and always, by loving other people.

We don't "love God" primarily by "being holy"—even though this is a repeated command of God in the Bible. If Jesus wanted to choose a greatest commandment based on how many times the idea is repeated in the Scriptures, "Be holy, for I am holy" would be a good candidate. But that's not what Jesus teaches. Holiness is important, but it is defined by love—not the other way around.

Nor do we "love God" primarily by "seeking truth"—even though truth is necessary and important. We are certainly to seek truth and speak truth, to gain knowledge and wisdom, but that is not the end of the matter. We can be absolutely right yet still be wrong, because we have not loved the other person as ourselves. (Hint: read 1 Corinthians 13 on "noisy gongs and clanging cymbals"!)

And we don't "love God" primarily by "experiencing God"—even though experiences of God can be good and beautiful and inspiring and enriching. For Jesus himself, it seems that regular, direct experience of God grounded everything he did—Jesus was known for his prayer life, after all (Luke 11:1–4). However, not even Jesus always sensed God's presence (Mark 15:34), and neither will we. Yet we are always to love others, in whom God is always present.

There are many good things, in fact, which could be candidates for demonstrating how—and how much—we love God. They may even be important, perhaps even necessary. But they are not the main thing.

This, then, is Jesus' radical teaching: *We "love God with our whole heart, soul, mind, and strength" primarily by "loving our neighbor as ourselves."*

Actually, that's not even the most radical bit, because for Jesus, "our neighbor" doesn't just mean those people with us, those people who live beside us, those who look and think and act like us.

Luke's gospel gives a different account than Matthew and Mark of Jesus and the extended Shema (Luke 10:25–37). In Luke's version, Jesus is asked, "What must I do to inherit eternal life?" That is, "What do I need to do to experience the fullness of God's life?"

Jesus turns the question back on the "expert in the Torah" who has approached him. "What is written in the Law?" asks Jesus. "What do you read there?" The questioner then gives the theologically correct answer (perhaps he'd heard Jesus before): "You shall love the Lord your God with all your heart and with all your soul and with all your strength and with all your mind and your neighbor as yourself." And Jesus responds by saying, "Do this, and you will live."

But the Torah expert doesn't stop there. Luke says he wants to "vindicate himself"—probably meaning he wants to assure himself that he's already loving God by loving his neighbor as himself. So he asks another question—"And who is my neighbor?"—hoping that Jesus will list all the people he's already loving: his family, his friends, the people next door. *Those people with us, those people who live beside us, those who look and think and act like us.*

Instead, Jesus tells a story.

> A man was going down from Jerusalem to Jericho and fell into the hands of robbers, who stripped him, beat him, and took off, leaving him half dead.
>
> Now by chance a priest was going down that road, and when he saw him he passed by on the other side. So likewise a Levite, when he came to the place and saw him, passed by on the other side.
>
> But a Samaritan while traveling came upon him, and when he saw him he was moved with compassion. He went to him and bandaged his wounds, treating them with oil and wine. Then he put him on his own animal, brought him to an inn, and took care of him. The next day he took out two denarii, gave them to the innkeeper, and said, "Take care of him, and when I come back I will repay you whatever more you spend." (Luke 10:30–35)

In the silence that follows, Jesus asks the Torah expert a final question: "Which of these three, do you think, was a neighbor to the man who fell into the hands of the robbers?" The man responds (you can almost hear the reluctance in his voice): "The one who showed him mercy." And Jesus concludes, "Go and do likewise" (vv. 36–37).

It's a well-known story of Jesus. And it's startlingly subversive.

Priests and Levites (temple assistants) were well respected by their fellow Jews in Jesus' day. Samaritans, by contrast, were not. They were seen as religious deviants, with their own temple and ways of worship. They were viewed as being of inferior pedigree, Israelite blood mixed with Gentile. And they were at times even looked upon as enemies, with hostilities occasionally breaking out between Samaritans and Jews.

Jesus thus subverts everyone's expectations by making a Samaritan the hero of the story. Jesus makes the stereotypical "other"—a stranger, even an enemy—simultaneously the example of neighbor love and the very neighbor whom his Jewish questioner is called to love.

For Jesus, "our neighbor" includes *anyone and everyone we encounter in life, including those who are different from us, those who are strangers to us, even those who intentionally oppose us and seek our harm—that is, our enemies.*

And loving our neighbor "as ourselves" means *loving these "others" as if their needs were our own, prioritizing their needs as if we ourselves had those needs.*

James, Peter, John, Paul—all the apostles got this (eventually). Those early Christians, those first followers of Jesus, all understood and accepted this teaching of Jesus that loving God and loving others were together the greatest commandment of God, the one thing that summed up everything else.

There's Paul in Romans 13:8–10: "Owe no one anything, except to love one another, for the one who loves another has fulfilled the law. The commandments, 'You shall not commit adultery; you shall not murder; you shall not steal; you shall not covet,' and any other commandment, are summed up in this word, 'You shall love your neighbor as yourself.' Love does no wrong to a neighbor; therefore, love is the fulfilling of the law."

Paul again in Galatians 5:14: "For the whole law is summed up in a single commandment, 'You shall love your neighbor as yourself.'"

There's James in James 2:8: "If you really fulfill the royal law according to the scripture, 'You shall love your neighbor as yourself,' you do well."

There's Peter in 1 Peter 4:8: "Above all, maintain constant love for one another, for love covers a multitude of sins."

There's John in 1 John 3:11: "For this is the message you have heard from the beginning, that we should love one another."

And John again in 1 John 4:21: "The commandment we have from him is this: those who love God must love their brothers and sisters also."

The early Christians not only understood and accepted this teaching, they really *got* Jesus' teaching on love. A letter from a Christian philosopher named Aristides to the emperor Hadrian, written about one hundred years after Jesus, describes how people knew they were Christians: by their love.

"The Christians," Aristides says, "comfort their oppressors and make them their friends; they do good to their enemies . . . . They love one another, and they do not turn away their esteem from widows; and they deliver the orphan from him who treats him harshly. And the one who has gives to him who has not, without boasting. And when they see a stranger, they take him in to their homes and rejoice over him as a very brother.

"Such, O King," Aristides concludes, "is the commandment of the law of the Christians, and such is their manner of life."[2]

Aristides is surely exaggerating to impress the emperor. Aristides was a Christian himself, eager to keep Christians on the good side of the governing authorities. Yet, even scaling back his description to a more modest degree, this fits with what we know from other sources of how Christians lived their lives in those first centuries after Jesus.

The early Christians *got* Jesus' teaching on love. Do we? Do we truly understand, accept, and seek to live out Jesus' love commandment as the most important thing we do, the overarching principle of all life?

CONFESSING THE LOVE COMMANDMENT

Within my denomination, Mennonite Church Canada, we have a confession of faith, a statement of what we believe as Mennonites.

I've always appreciated our confession of faith, or to give it its full title, the *Confession of Faith in a Mennonite Perspective*. It is one of the reasons I wanted to pastor in a Mennonite Church Canada church—our theological vision is one I value. I've also used our confession of faith in faith formation classes, which is one of the purposes it gives for itself in its opening pages. It's a good document.

But our denominational confession of faith is not infallible. This is highlighted by what the confession of faith says—or rather, doesn't say—about these commands to love God and love our neighbor. Surely we Mennonites who claim to uphold Jesus' teachings in a special way would have something good to say about what Jesus called "the first and greatest commandments" of God, which sum up the entire Law of Moses and all the Prophets!

However, our confession of faith doesn't make even a single reference to the twofold love commandment of Jesus. It talks about "love of enemy" a lot, and it mentions "love of neighbor" one time. But there's nothing about love of God and love of others being what Jesus considered the central teaching of Scripture.

It's a good thing our confession of faith also says in its opening pages that it "is subject to the authority of the Bible" and that it "should support but not replace the lived witness of faith"! The authority of the Bible on the command to love is unquestioned: it is the teaching of Jesus our Lord in the Gospels. And as for our lived witness of faith, I've seen enough love among our Mennonite churches (and yes, my non-Mennonite friends, among yours as well) to settle the question. We have been, as Paul puts it so wonderfully in 1 Thessalonians 4:9, "God-taught [*theodidaktos*] to love one another."

I have seen us welcome others like Jesus, open-handed and with open arms. I have seen us give ourselves for others like Jesus, open-handed and with open arms. But not always, and not fully. As a well-known confession of sin in the Anglican *Book of Common Prayer* puts it, "We have not loved you, God, with our whole heart; we have not loved our neighbors as ourselves."[3] Not always, and not fully.

We are often tempted to put something in the place of love as the primary way we show our undivided devotion to God. And when we do this, we've badly missed the point of Jesus' teaching.

READING THE BIBLE FOR LOVE

When we do this, we've also badly missed the whole point of the Bible. Jesus says that this extended Shema is the hook on which all the Law and the Prophets hang. This love for God by loving others sums up all the Law and the Prophets (Matthew 22:40).

In other words, the love commandment is the whole point of the Bible.

Here's what this means: *If our interpretation of a passage in the Bible leads us to not love another person in the way the foreigner good Samaritan loved that enemy Jew in need—open-handed, with open arms—then we are not reading the Bible rightly.*

History teaches us that we can justify a lot of terrible things by quoting the Bible. We can justify damaging, destructive things out of "love for God," out of undivided devotion to God. Racism, colonialism, genocide, slavery, crusades, inquisitions, and more have been committed by people committed to God. All have been defended by quoting the Bible.

But Jesus gives us a new hermeneutic. Jesus gives us a different way of reading the Bible: if we come up with an interpretation of a passage in the Bible that leads us to *not* love another person in the way Jesus loves us—open-handed, with open arms—we are not reading the Bible rightly.

Or, put in the positive, *when we read the Bible with Jesus, we learn to love God by loving others: neighbors, strangers, those who are different, even our enemies.*

New Testament scholar Scot McKnight calls this extended Shema the "Jesus Creed,"[4] and he suggests making this our own twice-daily prayer as followers of Jesus.

> Hear, O Israel: The LORD is our God, the LORD alone. Love the LORD your God with all your heart and with all your soul and with all your might, and love your neighbor as yourself. There is no commandment greater than these.

It's a terrific suggestion: confessing morning and evening what Jesus considered to be the most important teachings of the Torah. It's a great way to help us on our journey of reading the Bible with Jesus. Because this is truly a lifelong journey, learning to read the Bible with Jesus like this, learning to love God by loving others. But we can do it, one day at a time, because the Spirit of Jesus is in us and among us.

We can do it, one step at a time—by always simply loving the person in front of us.

THREE

Jubilee!

The spirit of the Lord GOD is upon me
  because the LORD has anointed me;
he has sent me to bring good news to the oppressed,
  to bind up the brokenhearted,
to proclaim liberty to the captives
  and release to the prisoners,
to proclaim the year of the LORD's favor.

—ISAIAH 61:1–2

LONGING FOR JUBILEE

Jesus held his mother's hand as they walked around the hill up toward Nazareth. They had been out since dawn gathering the last of the olives from old Uncle Simon's olive trees, and Mary now had a basketful held in her other hand against the sleeping baby slung in front of her: Jesus' baby sister, Mariam. Jesus' little brothers, James and Joses, skipped along behind them, stopping to prod insects and poke into burrows along the way. It was a beautiful late-autumn morning, perfect for picking olives—or for planting barley and wheat for spring.

They heard the men's voices before they rounded the bend: day laborers, sitting at the village entrance, waiting for someone to hire them to work those fields. These were men with families to feed and debts to pay.

"They're taxing the life out of us!" a deep voice growled. "And then they're taxing our death, too! If they could, they'd find a way to tax the resurrection!"

As the path turned Jesus could see the man: Ananias bar Matthias, standing in the middle of the path preaching to a small choir of three other men who sat off to the side.

"And the Romans aren't the worst of the lot!" Ananias continued, voice raising as heads nodded in agreement before him. "Those Judeans come up from Jerusalem with all their Roman coins and their fancy togas, and they take our land out from under us. They lease it back at double the price, and then throw us in jail when we can't pay!"

Mary called to James and Joses to come close. She squeezed Jesus' hand as she steered them to the other side of the narrow path. She knew Ananias was only blowing off steam; he wasn't saying anything he hadn't said a thousand times before. And everyone knew his anger was justified: he had himself just spent a month in debtor's prison. But sometimes his steam blew off with more than a little force, and Ananias was a big man.

Another man piped up just as they walked by, as if on cue: "We need a Jubilee, Ananias, a Jubilee!"

Jesus glanced at the man who had spoken. He wasn't sure of his name, but he had seen him around, both here and in Sepphoris, begging for work or for money. His leg had been injured years ago, and so he wouldn't be high on a landowner's list of laborers. Jesus wondered: did this man, too, have a family to support?

"A Jubilee!" Ananias snorted. "That's a legend, that is! No one here's ever seen a Jubilee, I'll tell you that much!"

Ananias's voice faded into the background as they entered the village. In a few minutes they were home, and Mary sighed as she set the basket of olives down and began to unwrap baby Mariam to nurse her.

"Mother," said Jesus, "what's a 'Jubilee'?"

Mary gave him a glance, still focused on her nursing baby. Once she had her settled, she gave Jesus her full attention.

"Jubilee is a special festival that lasts a whole year." She saw Jesus' raised eyebrows, and smiled. "Yes, my little Yeshu, imagine it! All debts forgiven, all land returned to its original owners, all prisoners and slaves set free! It's a year-long Sabbath: even the very earth rests in the presence of the Creator."

Jesus pondered this a moment. "It sounds like that song you sing, Imma," he said, reaching out to stroke the baby's cheek.

Mary looked at him in wonder. "Yes, Jesus, I suppose it does." She turned her head down toward little Mariam, content in her feeding. Softly she began to sing, as if in a lullaby:

My soul magnifies the LORD,
    and my spirit rejoices in God my Savior,

for God has looked with favor on the lowly state of
    God's servant . . .
God has brought down the powerful from their thrones,
    and lifted up the lowly;
God has filled the hungry with good things,
    and sent the rich away empty . . .

Her voice faded to a whisper. "Yes, that is Jubilee."

She shook her head, as if waking herself from a dream. "Well, there's at least one thing Ananias was right about," she declared.

"What's that, Imma?" Jesus asked, turning his head toward her intently.

"No one here has ever seen a Jubilee," she said sadly. "I'm not sure it's ever happened, anywhere. Not really."

JESUS' JUBILEE

In our exploration of how Jesus read his Bible, we've learned that Jesus didn't have a Bible like we do—a single book, holding all the writings that our Bibles have, available for each person to own and read for themselves. But at home and in the synagogue, in the village and its surrounding hillsides, Jesus did hear and learn the Torah, the Law of Moses, some of the Prophets like Isaiah, and some of the Writings like the Psalms.

And one of the texts that made a particular impression on Jesus was Isaiah 61. All of Isaiah, really—the Gospels are full of echoes of Isaiah's language and imagery, as we'll see later. But the first part of Isaiah 61 was a special text for Jesus. If he'd had an NIV Student Bible like I did as a young man, this passage would have been highlighted and underlined and well-worn from rereading.

The spirit of the Lord GOD is upon me,
 because the LORD has anointed me;
he has sent me to bring good news to the oppressed,
 to bind up the brokenhearted,
to proclaim liberty to the captives,
 and release to the prisoners;
to proclaim the year of the LORD's favor.

"The year of the LORD's favor." This is indeed that ancient promise of Jubilee, first given in the Law of Moses. In Leviticus 25, God's words to Moses on Mount Sinai include the instruction to hallow every fiftieth year and "proclaim liberty throughout the land to all its inhabitants" (v. 10). This Jubilee promise of liberation was recast for the exiled people of Israel to whom Isaiah prophesied (Isaiah 61), and recast again for the oppressed people of Galilee whom Jesus came to save.

For that's how Luke's gospel portrays it: Isaiah 61:1–2 is Jesus' personal mission statement.

In Luke 4:16–21, the grown-up Jesus comes back to his hometown synagogue in Nazareth. As a visitor, even seen by some as a rabbi, Jesus is invited to read and expound on the text from the Prophets. Jesus recites the opening verses of Isaiah 61—crucially stopping, as Luke tells it, after the line "to proclaim the year of the LORD's favor"—and then he announces, to the astonishment of all: "Today this scripture has been fulfilled in your hearing." Jesus has come to fulfill this Jubilee promise: good news for the poor, the downtrodden, the prisoners and slaves!

Later in Luke's gospel, Jesus again echoes these words. When the disciples of John the Baptist come to confirm that Jesus is the one who would bring about God's reign on earth, Jesus replies: "Go and tell John what you have seen and heard: the blind receive their sight; the lame walk; those with a skin disease are cleansed; the deaf hear; the dead are raised; the poor have good news brought to them" (7:18–22).

When we hear these words of Jesus, we often spiritualize them. We take them figuratively and then apply them spiritually. The "poor," we say, are the "spiritually impoverished," those who need a personal relationship with God. The "oppressed," the "captives," the "prisoners"—for us, these refer to "spiritual oppression" or "captivity" or "imprisonment," to individual people needing to be freed from the guilt of their personal sins.

But that's not how people in Jesus' day would have heard those words—at least not primarily, and not entirely. Yes, Jesus speaks much of sins and forgiveness and the need for a devoted, trusting relationship with God. But for Jesus, individual sin and salvation is bound up with much larger realities. In Jesus' way of thinking, we all need liberation from sinful, evil powers that manifest in structures and systems in society. Put differently, this poverty, this oppression, this imprisonment and enslavement, is both literal and figurative, both physical and spiritual.

We have learned the greatest commandment of God at the heart of Jesus' teaching: we are called to love God with undivided devotion, and we are called to do this by loving others with generous compassion. But this love is not simply about loving God as individuals, and then loving individuals in the way of God—as important as that is. According to Jesus, *this love also shows itself in a pursuit of justice and peace and life for all people, especially the most vulnerable and disadvantaged.*

The philosopher and activist Cornel West has frequently put it this way: "Justice is what love looks like in public."[1] That's exactly right.

And that's what Jesus' Jubilee mission is all about. To borrow Jesus' words from Matthew 6:33, in following Jesus we are to "seek first God's kingdom and God's righteousness"—God's *dikaiosunē*, God's way of justice.

GOD'S REIGN AND GOD'S JUSTICE

The language of "God's kingdom" is heard often on Jesus' lips in the Gospels. In fact, it is how Mark's gospel summarizes Jesus' message: "Jesus came to Galilee proclaiming the good news of God and saying, 'The time is fulfilled, and the kingdom of God has come near'" (1:14–15).

The ears of Jesus' Galilean listeners would have perked up at that. They knew firsthand about kingdoms, and they longed for God's kingdom to come.

They knew about the Roman Empire, that kingdom that had spread all round the Mediterranean Sea, a kingdom that brought peace and prosperity for Rome and its citizens through the conquest and crucifixion and colonization of others.

They knew about Herod's kingdom, a puppet kingdom of Rome, ensuring Roman peace and prosperity for the few by maintaining control of the many.

They knew about the Hasmonean kingdom more than a century earlier, a glorious time of relative independence from foreign empires after Judas Maccabee and his brothers had brought them liberation through armed revolt.

And they also knew about God's kingdom, promised in Isaiah and the other Prophets, a coming reign of God on earth bringing about true justice and lasting peace and flourishing life for God's people.

And so when Jesus came invoking Isaiah and bringing "good news to the oppressed" and proclaiming "the year of the LORD's favor"—they knew what Jesus was getting at: God was coming to reign, and this reign of God would mean justice for all who were hungering and thirsting for it.

GOD'S REIGN AND ECONOMIC JUSTICE

This loving-God-by-loving-others way of Jesus, this kingdom-justice way of Jesus, this Jubilee of Jesus, includes economic justice.

"Economic justice" means everyone having their basic needs met, and even an equitable distribution of wealth (not necessarily equal, mind you, but equitable or fair).

For some, the words "economic justice" smack of a liberal agenda, but economic justice is simply the biblical vision of a just society. It's already there in the Torah, which called on Israel to provide for and protect the rights of the poor, the widows, orphans, and foreigners among them.

According to Deuteronomy 24, the wealthy were to leave the corners of their fields unharvested and the last of the fruit on the vine so that the poor could come and harvest for themselves (24:19–21).

According to Deuteronomy 23–24, the wealthy were not to charge interest—any interest at all—on loans they gave to their fellow Israelites. They were not to take a poor person's cloak overnight as a pledge against a loan, because that was the only covering they had to stay warm (23:19; 24:12–13).

According to Deuteronomy 24, the wealthy were to pay their workers every day the work was done, because, as the Law says, "they are poor and their livelihood depends on [their wages]; otherwise they might cry to the LORD against you, and you would incur guilt" (24:15).

According to Leviticus 19, judges were specifically commanded to judge fairly, not to favor the rich and powerful over the poor and powerless—or even the other way around (19:15).

And according to Leviticus 25, every fifty years, in the year of Jubilee, all property was to return to its original owners—a reset button on property ownership so that no family would be without economic security forever. This was to keep the rich from getting obscenely wealthy at the expense of the working, debt-ridden poor (25:8–17).

This radical call for economic justice is woven through the rest of the Bible. This was one of the prophets' most frequent rebukes, that the rich were getting richer at the expense of the poor. In fact, this is what Ezekiel called "the guilt of Sodom"—not anything to do with sex, but rather that the people of Sodom "had pride, excess of food, and prosperous ease but did not aid the poor and needy" (Ezekiel 16:49).

And this radical call for economic justice was a key feature of Jesus' teaching and ministry.

"Woe to you who are rich," Jesus cried, not mincing any words, but "blessed are you who are poor, for yours is the kingdom of God" (Luke 6:20, 24).

You who live like the rich man while ignoring the poor man at your gates—God will judge you, Jesus warned (Luke 16:19–31).

If you pursue wealth ahead of God's reign, you are serving a different God, Jesus declared, and you might need to sell everything you have to follow Jesus and find true life (Matthew 6:24; 19:16–30).

And all Jesus' free healing and generous feeding of the poor peasants of Galilee? This undermined the whole system of economic privilege built by the wealthy and the powerful. It's also simply what Jesus called his followers to do: feed the hungry, welcome the stranger, clothe the naked, care for the sick (Matthew 25:31–46).

GOD'S REIGN AND SOCIAL JUSTICE

This loving-God-by-loving-others way of Jesus, this kingdom-justice way of Jesus, this Jubilee of Jesus, includes, then, what we today call social justice.

"Social justice" also gets a hard knock in some Christian circles. That's really, really *weird*, to be honest, since Christianity has always sought to focus on providing for the poor, welcoming the stranger, and caring for the sick. Even when Christian institutions have been at their most corrupt in history, when the church hasn't been doing these things all that much, no Christian would have imagined criticizing these acts as not central to Christian faith or even outright condemning them as unchristian. Yet that's what we hear sometimes today.

But that perspective doesn't match up with Jesus. What we today call "social justice"—lifting up the poor, centering those on the margins, protecting those most vulnerable to harm—is simply what Jesus called "loving your neighbor as yourself." What we today call social justice is simply what Jesus called "the kingdom of God and God's righteousness," which we are to seek first above all other empires and dominions.

At bottom, these social justice concerns are about power, or the lack of it—the ability of people to shape their circumstances for the better.

There are many ways we gain this kind of power, or lose it. Wealth gives us greater power over our circumstances; poverty can make us powerless to change them. Social status and social connections give us influence over others, and thus help from others in dealing with our difficult circumstances; those without status or connections don't have this power.

Sometimes we can do things to gain power for ourselves, but we can also obtain this kind of power through no effort of our own—even if we think it's because of our hard work or ingenuity. We might inherit our wealth. We might be born into status or have connections through our parents. Or we might simply be of the socially dominant ethnicity, language, sex, or gender. As a white, straight, middle-aged man, I have more power to change my circumstances than many others in Canada—even if I'm not among the wealthiest!

Jesus modeled loving his neighbor as himself—prioritizing their needs as if he himself had those needs—primarily by focusing on those his society considered "the last," "the least," and "the lost" (Matthew 20:1–16; 25:31–46; Luke 15). Those without wealth or status, those outside the central social circles of the community—that is, those without power.

This—empowering the powerless—is at the heart of what's known as social justice, and it's at the heart of Jesus' Jubilee mission.

GOD'S REIGN AND POLITICS

This loving-God-by-loving-others way of Jesus, this kingdom-justice way of Jesus, this Jubilee of Jesus, is therefore deeply political.

I don't mean it's political in the way we often think of politics today. "Politics" as a general term simply describes how human groups organize themselves and make decisions for the common good. However, when we think of politics today, we might instead think of partisan fights over power for our own self-interest. I mean the *opposite* of that, actually.

Jesus' message was thoroughly political. Jesus talked about "kingdom" all the time in a world of emperors and kings—that's about as political as you can get! Rome proclaimed a "gospel" of "peace" through the emperor as "savior" and "lord." When Jesus used those same words but in a different way, everyone heard the political critique in them.

But Jesus couldn't have cared less which specific person was in charge in Jerusalem or Tiberias or Caesarea or Rome, the political centers of his world. The next emperor might be better than the last, but he would still be the head of a profoundly unjust system. And Jesus wasn't lobbying for prosperity and security for himself and his family and all those who were just like him. The politics of Jesus aren't about partisan fights over power for our own self-interest.

Rather, the politics of Jesus are about loving God by loving others, seeking first God's kingdom-justice for all, especially for those who have been pushed down in society as "the least of these" or "the last of all." And this has tremendous significance for politics in the generic sense I named earlier: how we organize ourselves as a society and make decisions for the common good.

The politics of Jesus can work through the politics of the world. Indeed, often they must, if we are going to truly love others by prioritizing their needs as if they were our own. We should use whatever political means are at our disposal—those appropriate for followers of Jesus, that is—to ensure that all of us, and especially those our society diminishes or decenters, can live in true justice and lasting peace and flourishing life.

But it's ultimately irrelevant for us as followers of Jesus what nation we live in. Ultimately it doesn't matter who governs us. We are to love God by loving others, we are to pursue God's just and peaceable reign, Jesus' vision of Jubilee, regardless of whoever's in power and whatever political system we find ourselves in.

OUR JUBILEE?

All this makes me wonder: What might Jesus' Jubilee look like in our communities?

How can we "proclaim the year of the LORD's favor" right where we are? How can we "bring good news to the poor" and "recovery of sight to the blind" (Luke 4:18) in our towns and cities, in our immediate neighborhood? How can we "proclaim release to the captives" and "let the oppressed go free" in our twenty-first-century world?

Who are the most vulnerable-to-harm and disadvantaged among us, the most downtrodden and broken among us, the most powerless among us—in our church, in our city, in our country, in our world—and how can we walk with them in love toward Jesus' justice-bringing Jubilee?

Some difficult conversations are happening among us as Christians, in our churches and denominations—we can't deny that. Conversations about sexuality and gender, about rights and freedoms, about politics and the public role of religion. And these difficult conversations are taking their toll on us, polarizing and dividing us—we can't deny that either.

But we as Christians must not lose sight of what matters most: following Jesus, particularly by obeying Jesus' greatest commandment and living out Jesus' kingdom mission. Jesus calls us to rally around him, to walk in his way of love—showing undivided devotion to God by showing generous compassion for others—and so to pursue God's justice and peace for all. This is what we are called to as Christians and churches, this above all else.

So let's love whoever walks in our doors—including one another! And then let's go out our doors and love whomever we encounter along the way, even seeking out the most vulnerable and disadvantaged, the most downtrodden and broken among us, the most powerless among us. Let's walk in loving solidarity with them into Jesus' Jubilee, a world where there is true justice and lasting peace.

Yes, this is a hard road—it is a narrow way, Jesus says, and few find it (Matthew 7:13–14). It requires sacrifice in solidarity with the poor, the disabled, the marginalized, the mistreated. And it will lead to opposition—people with power and privilege often don't like when they have to give up some of their power to empower others. Still, this sacrifice and opposition shouldn't surprise us. It is the way of the cross, Jesus says, denying ourselves and taking up our cross daily and following him (Luke 9:23–25).

But this way of the cross, Jesus also says, is the only way that leads to life—for us, for others, for all people, and for all creation.

FOUR

A Secret Message

Go and say to this people:

"Keep listening, but do not comprehend;
keep looking, but do not understand."
Make the mind of this people dull,
    and stop their ears,
    and shut their eyes,
so that they may not look with their eyes
    and listen with their ears
and comprehend with their minds
    and turn and be healed."

—ISAIAH 6:9–10

JESUS' FAVORITE BIBLE BOOKS

Here's an interesting fact: there are certain books of the Old Testament that Jesus in the Gospels never refers to, and there are certain books of the Old Testament that Jesus refers to often. This is true, in fact, of the whole New Testament.

As much as I love both Ecclesiastes and Esther, for example, Jesus showed little interest in either of them. But Jesus' favorite books of the Bible? The Psalms, Isaiah, and Deuteronomy. If you add Genesis and Exodus into the mix, you've got the five most-quoted books of the Old Testament in the New Testament, and by a pretty fair margin over other Old Testament books.

Even more than just which Old Testament books Jesus or his apostles quoted most often is *the way* in which those books are quoted. Jesus and the first Christians refer to their Scriptures, our Old Testament, using certain patterns, and those patterns are telling.

Take Leviticus, for instance. Leviticus was very important to most Jews in Jesus' day, with all its commands about blood sacrifices and holy living and unclean foods and unclean people. But Jesus directly quotes only two verses from all of Leviticus.

One is Leviticus 24:20: "Eye for eye, tooth for tooth; the injury inflicted is the injury to be suffered," which Jesus reads not in the letter of the law but in its spirit. He moves beyond the literal commandment—which reads like a recipe for retaliation but was in reality intended to limit revenge—toward radical nonviolence (see Matthew 5:38–39). The other is Leviticus 19:18, "Love your neighbor as yourself," which, as we've seen, Jesus uses to explain what true "love of God" looks like.

Most of the commands in Leviticus Jesus himself follows but doesn't teach on. When he does teach on them—as he does in Mark 7:1–23 on unclean foods—he again follows the pattern of reading beneath the letter of the law to discern the spirit of the law. We'll explore his motivation for this in the next chapter.

And sometimes, when an idea from Leviticus is expanded in later scriptures, Jesus prefers the later scripture to the passage in Leviticus. Like the whole Jubilee idea that we just explored. Jubilee first appears in Leviticus 25—yet Jesus' Jubilee quotation isn't from Leviticus but Isaiah. In other words, Jesus read Leviticus through the lens of Isaiah.

The early Christians, following Jesus' example and in line with some other Jewish groups of the day, absolutely loved Isaiah. It's not just that Isaiah gets quoted a lot in the New Testament. It's that the very language and ideas of Isaiah permeate the whole New Testament. All that talk of "gospel" and God's "reign" and "salvation" and "justice" and "peace" and more? All that comes from, or is heavily influenced by, the book of Isaiah.

So here's a practical bit of advice for us: if we truly want to read the Bible with Jesus, we should put this book down, pick up our Bibles, and read through all of Isaiah. Or, if that's too much at once, we can read through Isaiah 40–66, where those key New Testament ideas are most thick on the ground.

Because if we want to read the Bible with Jesus—really, if we want to understand Jesus himself—we need to become well acquainted with the prophets Isaiah.

SOWING THE WORD

Shortly after dawn, Jesus and Joseph took to the narrow path that wound down the steep hillside on its way to Sepphoris. Joseph had work this day in the city—a construction boom was going on there, what with the younger Herod's desire to remake

Sepphoris into "the ornament of the Galilee"—and Joseph thought Jesus might like to come along. Jesus was now nine years old, after all, old enough to take some interest in Joseph's trade.

They walked in comfortable silence together, the slap of their sandals on the hard path a steady rhythm filled only with the music of birds in the scattered trees along the way. The path before them was mottled in light and shadow as the sun slowly rose through the eastern hills.

As they rounded the bottom of the hill, a scene opened up before them, a scene fit for one of the frescoes Joseph had described in the homes of the wealthy where he sometimes worked.

The valley opposite was radiant in the morning sun. The subtle slope had been tilled to a golden brown that seemed to drink in the sun's rays. Here and there, the rocky underlay burst out, glowing silver in the sunlight. Pockets of small trees accented the image with their shades of green and brown. A handful of sowers were weaving their way across the tilled earth, scattering their seeds in a wide arc around them, singing as they swayed to the rhythm of their work.

Jesus and Joseph paused a moment, taking in the scene. Then, without a word, they continued on their journey.

It was, as usual, Jesus who broke the silence between them. "Abba, those sowers across the valley: they do the work of God, don't they?"

Joseph glanced sideways at the boy without breaking his stride. It always caught him up short when Jesus called him "Abba." Father. It seemed an act of grace on Jesus' part, as if Jesus knew the stories people told about his birth yet insisted on honoring Joseph anyway.

"They do God's work as much as I do, I suppose," Joseph said. "All honest labor is God's labor." He took a longer look at Jesus. "But you know that. I suspect you mean something else."

Jesus shrugged his shoulders and smiled. "Maybe I do. It's just this: God gives the seed for us to sow, but we must do the sowing. We till the soil, or as much as we can do, and then we scatter the seed. We are laborers together with God, you might say."

Jesus tilted his head for a moment, thinking some more. Something about the pose caused a fierce love for his son—this son who wasn't his son—to well up in Joseph.

"But in the end, I suppose," Jesus concluded, "we can't actually make the seed grow. That's up to God."

Joseph raised his eyebrows at that. "Are you so sure, Jesus?"

Jesus looked at Joseph in surprise. "What do you mean?"

"Think of the Prophet Isaiah," Joseph said. "He was called by God to speak God's word to the people, yet God told Isaiah no one would listen to him. God's message—God's seed—requires good soil for it to take root and grow." He paused. "It's not only up to God, then. The seed can only grow in open and receptive hearts."

"That is true, Abba," Jesus said. If he was surprised that Joseph had moved from seeds of grain to messages from God, he did not show it. "Sometimes the people who most need to hear God's word are the least likely to receive it. And yet"—Jesus cast a sly smile toward Joseph—"did not Isaiah also say that

As the rain and the snow come down from heaven,
    and do not return there until they have watered the earth,
making it bring forth and sprout,
    giving seed to the sower and bread to the eater,

so shall my word be that goes out from my mouth;
>   it shall not return to me empty,
> but it shall accomplish that which I purpose,
>   and succeed in the thing for which I sent it?

Joseph stopped short, his breath caught in his throat. Jesus stepped a few more paces, then stopped and turned to look at him. Jesus' face was illuminated in the morning sun, as if every feature were traced in divine glory.

Joseph smiled at his son, this son who was not his son. "Indeed, Jesus," he said softly, an edge of holy fear on his words, "that is so."

Jesus smiled in return, grabbed Joseph's hand in his, and together they continued on the way, singing together the song of the sowers, the song of Isaiah the word-sowing prophet:

> You shall go out with joy,
>   and be led forth with peace;
> the mountains and the hills
>   shall break forth before you,
> there will be shouts of joy
>   and all the trees of the field will clap their hands.

"THOSE WHO HAVE EARS TO HEAR"

The book of Isaiah was written by at least two people.

The original Isaiah prophesied around 700 years before Jesus, about 125 years before the first time Jerusalem and the temple were destroyed by the Babylonians in 586 BCE. His oracles are found in Isaiah 1–39. This Isaiah chastised Judah and other nations both for their alliances with oppressive empires and for their warmongering politics. He rebuked them for their social injustice and their oppression of the poor. He also gave some of the most memorable oracles about the coming reign of the Messiah: the son of David who would bring true justice and lasting peace on earth.

Second Isaiah, as scholars call them (there might have been more than one), lived a couple hundred years later, after the fall of Jerusalem, during Judah's exile in Babylon. Their oracles are found in Isaiah 40–66. This Isaiah comforted the people with promises of God's reign to come, Jubilee unleashed on earth, calling this "good news" or "gospel." They described a "servant"—some thought Israel itself, others the prophet himself, but Christians later said Jesus—a servant who would bring this kingdom Jubilee about through his teaching, his lifting up of the weak, and even his own suffering.

Both Isaiahs were brilliant: theological geniuses filled with God's Spirit to speak God's words in their day to those who had ears to hear.

But that was the problem: most people in their days did not have ears to hear. In original Isaiah's day, when Judah was prospering, no one wanted to hear words of woe. In second Isaiah's day, when Judah was beginning to settle in a foreign land, no one wanted to hear a message of return from exile through suffering.

And so both Isaiahs spoke in oracles rich with imagery and metaphor and even riddle. Those who were ready to hear could hear and understand, and those who weren't willing to hear would listen and be condemned by their own hardness of heart.

Jesus picked up on this for his own ministry, claiming that his own listeners were as "hard of hearing" as Isaiah's had been. So Jesus spoke in parables, stories rich with everyday imagery and provocative metaphor and even some riddle.

Like Jesus' parable of the sower in Matthew 13:3–9.

Listen!

A sower went out to sow. And as he sowed, some seeds fell on a path, and the birds came and ate them up. Other seeds fell on rocky ground, where they did not have much soil, and they sprang up quickly, since they had no depth of soil. But when the sun rose, they were scorched, and since they had no root, they withered away. Other seeds fell among thorns, and the thorns grew up and choked them. Other seeds fell on good soil and brought forth grain, some a hundredfold, some sixty, some thirty.

If you have ears, hear!

Jesus might simply be describing an everyday scene in Galilee, much like the fictional scene I painted earlier in this chapter. Yet we are bidden to listen, to pay close attention, even to ask questions of the story, until we find understanding. Who is the sower? What is the seed? What are the different types of soil?

Jesus doesn't often interpret his own parables for his disciples, but this one he does, as if giving us a template for understanding these story-riddles he's so fond of.

Hear, then, the parable of the sower.

When anyone hears the word of the kingdom and does not understand it, the evil one comes and snatches away what is sown in the heart; this is what was sown on the path. As for what was sown on rocky ground, this is the one who hears the word and immediately receives it with joy, yet such a person has no root but endures only for a while, and when trouble or persecution arises on account of the word, that person immediately falls away. As for what was sown among thorns, this is the one who hears the word, but the cares of this age and the lure of wealth choke the word, and it yields nothing. But as for what was sown on good soil, this is the one who hears the word and understands it, who indeed bears fruit and yields in one case a hundredfold, in another sixty, and in another thirty. (Matthew 13:18–23)

The seed is "the word of the kingdom," Jesus' good news of God's reign come near. The sower isn't named, but it's someone who spreads this good-news message around—certainly Jesus himself, but his followers also. Each of the four soils is a person's "heart," shaped by various life choices and circumstances.

A heart unable to appreciate the significance of the good news of God's reign.

A heart unable, or perhaps unwilling, to explore the depths of a life following Jesus.

A heart unwilling, or maybe unable, to root out soul-choking desires for wealth and power and other such things this world cares about.

A heart both able and willing to appreciate God's good news, to walk in Jesus' way, and to remove the obstacles that keep us from living out Jesus' way of love.

In the three gospels where this parable is told (Matthew 13, Mark 4, and Luke 8), Jesus quotes Isaiah 6 between his telling of the parable of the sower and his interpretation of it. This parable, therefore, underlines and highlights the point of Isaiah 6.

Those who are ready to hear Jesus' gospel of the kingdom, his message of love bringing God's life-giving reign, will hear and understand, and this message will take root and grow and bear fruit. But those who, because of their privilege or their power or their greed or their pride or their fear, aren't willing to hear Jesus' message? They will listen and condemn themselves through their own hardness of heart.

This is a difficult truth; but it is the simple truth. Jesus' message is a public proclamation, there for all to hear! Yet it is also a secret message, accessible only to those who are willing to set aside their egos in order to save themselves and others.

However, this never stopped Jesus from preaching the gospel of God's reign. He continued on throughout the villages of Galilee and beyond, even to the edge of the Gentiles, denouncing injustice and oppression and all sins of harm, yet throwing parties for repentant sinners and sharing table with all the very last people anyone would want to eat with. He persisted in proclaiming the message of God's reign of justice and peace come to earth through open-handed, open-hearted, self-giving, suffering love—and that scattering of seed sometimes fell on good soil, took root, and grew, and bore much fruit.

After all, God's word *will* accomplish that which God intends for it.

And so we follow Jesus in scattering the seed of God's reign. We persist. We keep on.

We keep on speaking truth to power whenever and however we can, calling for justice and pushing for peace. We keep on standing up to the bullies of our world, standing with the bullied, whether in our schools or in our workplaces or in our society or on the other side of the world. We keep on reaching out to all our neighbors, including those who are different from us, who are strangers to us, who are even enemies of us, seeking mutual understanding and the common good.

We keep on forgiving the sinful, lifting up the shamed, seeking the lost and lonely, healing the wounded, feeding the hungry, extending the table to break bread with more and more people. We keep on proclaiming and living out the good news of God's love, regardless of whether the message is truly heard, regardless of whether our own love is spurned. This is the way of Isaiah, and it's the way of Jesus.

HEARING THE TRUTH SLANT

Another dimension of Jesus' teaching is also important for us to understand here. Because Jesus' teaching comes to us in parable, in indirect metaphor and subversive story—telling the truth "slant," as the poet Emily Dickinson put it[1]—we must always recognize that we don't own Jesus' teaching, and we can't control it. We don't have the corner on Jesus' teaching, or on how to live it out.

This is true of the whole Bible, actually, which is filled with poetry and proverb and song and story. Jesus—and even the Bible as a whole—teaches us in indirect, slanted ways that require much pondering and deep soul-searching.

This means that if we want to hear Jesus' teaching well, and if we want to read the Bible with Jesus, we need to come to it humbly. We need to open our own hearts to receive God's word, the gospel of the kingdom. We need to be open to what God wants to do in us, even if this means changing us in uncomfortable ways. And we need to be open to different, even fresh ways of hearing and living out this word from God.

At the end of Matthew's collection of Jesus' parables, in Matthew 13, Jesus concludes with these words: "Every scribe who has become a disciple in the kingdom of heaven is like the master of a household who brings out of his treasure what is new and what is old" (13:52). Once we are trained in Jesus' kingdom teachings, we can bring out important truths that are as old as the hills, but we will also continue to discover important truths that are as new as each day's dawn.

I don't know about you, but I love the idea that there is always more to discover about walking in the way of Jesus.

FIVE

Mercy, Not Sacrifice

For I desire steadfast love [mercy] and not sacrifice,
the knowledge of God rather than burnt offerings.

—HOSEA 6:6

RABBI JESUS

The last chapter introduced us to Jesus as teacher, Jesus as a rabbi. Like other rabbis of Jesus' day, he taught in parables, story-riddles based in everyday life but with a deeper meaning—often a surprising or subversive one.

There were many such rabbis in Jesus' day throughout Galilee and neighboring Judea. The title of *rabbi* for teachers of Torah was not formalized then, as it would be in the centuries that followed. There were a variety of ways one could study the Torah, and a variety of teachers on offer. Priests taught the Torah, as one might expect, but there were also laypeople like the Pharisees who were devoted to the study of Torah and shared their learning as rabbis with their own disciples. Hillel and Shammai, the two great rabbis we met earlier, were Pharisees.

We don't know a lot for sure about how all these rabbis operated in Jesus' day. However, we can say a few things with some confidence. Rabbis were Jewish teachers of Torah, the Law of Moses. Whether priests or laypeople, they had studied the Torah significantly. They memorized large portions of it, whether in Hebrew or in Aramaic or Greek translation, and they were familiar with the main interpretations of the Torah. These rabbis, as teachers, naturally had students—disciples, they were called.

In Jerusalem, where it seems most certain that there were formal schools for studying the Torah, this education would have begun at a primary level for boys (no girls allowed) at around age five or six. These boys would have simply learned the written Torah: how to read the Hebrew text and memorizing significant parts of it. Around age ten, these boys would begin to learn the teachings of prior rabbis like Hillel and

Shammai, memorizing them orally. By age thirteen or so, the more gifted of these students might have the opportunity to become disciples of the most learned rabbis.

That's in first-century Jerusalem. In Galilee, and especially in small villages like Nazareth, primary education (learning to read the written Torah) may have been done at the synagogue, with a local elder as teacher, or perhaps in the home, the father as teacher. Secondary education (learning the oral Torah, the teachings of the rabbis) would have been unusual but possible if a rabbi were available—like my fictional Rabbi Eleazar in an earlier chapter.

Even Jesus' critics in the Gospels acknowledge that Jesus was a rabbi (for instance, see Matthew 22:16). Jesus knew the Torah, both written and at least some oral, even if he hadn't formally studied it in Jerusalem (John 7:15). And as a traveling rabbi, an itinerant teacher, he gathered to himself disciples to learn his teaching of Torah, to learn firsthand his way of living out the Torah, his way of love.

Discipleship in Jesus' day was a communal effort. Rabbis would often gather disciples (plural) who would form a learning community around their teacher—working out together what their rabbi's teaching meant for them, how it should be lived out in their world. Even the rabbis discussed and debated among themselves what the Torah meant and how previous rabbis had interpreted it. This communal learning, even communal discussion and debate, was certainly common among the disciples of Jesus—as the Gospels, Acts, and New Testament Epistles attest.

Jesus' first disciples were an uninspiring group, at first glance, not like the typical disciples of those learned rabbis in Jerusalem. There were the twelve: Simon Peter, James, John, and others. All men, as would be expected in those days, some of them fishermen and others likely trained in a trade, probably all with at most a primary education. Yet there were others beyond the twelve, including women. Luke's gospel, for instance, portrays Mary of Bethany as the ideal disciple, sitting at her rabbi's feet, learning his Torah-teaching (10:38–42).

The idea of *discipleship* carries on beyond the Gospels. In Acts, Luke uses the language of "disciples" to continue to describe believers in Jesus. In fact, "disciples," or those who follow "the Way," is Luke's favorite description of Christians— including the only time a woman is explicitly called a disciple in the New Testament (Acts 9:36). (While it might seem strange to us today, "Christians" was not what the early Jesus-followers called themselves but rather how non-Christians referred to them; see Acts 11:26; 26:28.)

There's good reason, therefore, for us to carry on thinking of ourselves as Christians this way: we are disciples of Rabbi Jesus, our Teacher, learning together how to read the Scriptures, learning together Jesus' way of loving God by loving others.

"MERCY, NOT SACRIFICE": HOSEA 6

And in Matthew 9:13, Jesus our Teacher gives us some homework.

"Go and learn what this means," he says to the Pharisees, the Really Religious folk (if I'd been there, that would be me, with all my theological training and religious devotion): "I desire mercy, not sacrifice."

So let's do this homework together, starting with the prophet Hosea, where this quote comes from.

In Hosea's day, some 750 years before Jesus, Israel was prosperous and successful, but they were awash in idolatry and injustice. They had turned to literal idols, but the idols of power and wealth were even greater. The rich got richer on the backs of the poor. The powerful secured power by oppressing the weak.

And yet Israel continued the prescribed religious rituals—prescribed by God in the Law of Moses, of course—because they believed this maintained their righteous standing before God. The priests were puppets of the powerful, play-acting their way through the Torah. They sacrificed bulls and sheep and goats to God on the altar in the temple in Jerusalem—and then, when they left the holy place, they catered to the whims of the wealthy at the expense of the poor.

But God would rather have God's people living in simple *hesed*—Hebrew for "steadfast love," "loving-kindness," "mercy"—than have them do all the prescribed rituals of the Law put together. God would rather have God's people living in love—devotion to God expressed through compassion and care for others—than have them sacrifice all the bulls and sheep and goats in the world.

Other prophets echoed this sentiment, sometimes with very strong words.

A psalm of David: "Sacrifice and offering you [the LORD] do not desire, but you have given me an open ear [signifying obedience]. Burnt offering and sin offering you have not required" (Psalm 40:6).

An oracle of Micah: "'With what shall I come before the LORD, and bow myself before God on high? Shall I come before him with burnt offerings, with calves a year old? Will the LORD be pleased with thousands of rams, with ten thousands of rivers of oil? Shall I give my firstborn for my transgression, the fruit of my body for the sin of my soul?' He has told you, O mortal, what is good, and what does the LORD require of you but to do justice, and to love kindness, and to walk humbly with your God?" (Micah 6:6–8).

An indictment of Jeremiah: "For from the least to the greatest of them, everyone is greedy for unjust gain; and from prophet to priest, everyone deals falsely . . . . Your burnt offerings are not acceptable, nor are your sacrifices pleasing to me" (Jeremiah 6:13–20).

Or, as God says to Israel through the prophet Hosea: "I desire mercy, not sacrifice."

I don't know about you, but I'm good with that. As much as I love my religious rituals, and as rich as those rituals are, I'd love to be free from feeling obligated to do religion in just the right way. I'd love to be free to do religion in a way that's *free*, you know? I'd love to be free to do religion in a way that focuses on the stuff that matters most, like "doing justice and loving mercy and walking humbly with God," like "loving God by loving others."

"MERCY, NOT SACRIFICE": MATTHEW 9

We take that bit of homework back to Jesus our Teacher, and he turns to us again: "Go and learn what this means: I desire mercy, not sacrifice."

So let's go deeper. Let's check out the context where Jesus first quotes this scripture text—Matthew 9—and consider why Jesus said what he said when he said it.

There's Jesus, eating with sinners, and the Really Religious (again, that would be me) don't like it. Their concern is about holiness, about maintaining purity. For them this is the prescribed sacrifice according to the Law. It's what the Bible calls for.

Religious purity is a foreign concept to most of us. When we see the language of "clean" and "unclean" in the Bible, perhaps the first thing that comes to mind is hygiene. But even the cleansing rituals in the Bible that involve water are not about washing the dirt off our bodies; rather, they are talking about religious purity.

Essentially, religious purity for first-century Jews was about being set apart, or "holy," as God's people. Its primary focus was on being properly prepared to come near to God's presence in the temple in Jerusalem. This was critical to Jews of that day, being able to enter the temple to offer sacrifices for sins or in thanksgiving to God.

However, in Jesus' day this need to be cleansed or purified was extended to other sacred moments, like entering the synagogue to worship or to study the Torah. So at the temple in Jerusalem and at synagogues in Galilee, ritual baths (*mikva'ot*) were available for people to wash themselves.

Purity was not about morality, or at least not the way we typically think of morality. Jews could become ritually impure simply by living life, literally from birth to death. A woman was considered impure after having a baby (Leviticus 12). A man was considered impure after non-coital emission of semen (Leviticus 15:1–18). Anyone who touched a corpse, such as preparing a loved one's body for burial, would likewise be unclean (Numbers 31:19–20). So it was normal to see people going to wash themselves at the village *mikvah*, and it was expected that Galileans making their annual trek to Jerusalem for Passover, say, would need both to bathe and then to sacrifice in order to cleanse their year's worth of impurities.

Yet some impurities did carry strong moral overtones. Eating pork or other unclean foods was unthinkable for a devout Jew, for instance (Leviticus 11). For many Jews in Jesus' day, eating food with a Gentile in their home (because one could not be sure the food was kosher, or clean) was also viewed in what we might consider moral terms. And for at least some, like the Really Religious in Matthew 9, a devout Jew concerned with proper purity should not even eat with those Jews who were deemed sinners, those who were considered not to be properly following the Torah.

However, Jesus' concern is about mercy, about showing steadfast love, compassionate care, especially to those who most need it. This is the greater pursuit. This is God's greater desire.

Jesus doesn't neglect the reality of sin—Jesus calls all sinners to repentance, remember? "Repent, for the kingdom of God is come near" (Mark 1:15)—that's Jesus' basic message in a nutshell. But Jesus turns the whole notion of sin on its head. When we push down and push aside the most broken, the most vulnerable, the most marginalized—and especially when we justify this by appealing to holiness before God—this is the greater sin.

It's no surprise, then, that this is especially what got Jesus' blood boiling—as we see in Matthew 23.

"The scribes and the Pharisees sit on Moses's seat," Jesus says, affirming their widespread authority, "therefore, do whatever they teach you and follow it" (23:2–3). Contrary to much popular Christian thinking today, Jesus never rejected the Pharisees' teaching or authority. Jesus' broad generalizations here did not reflect the attitudes and actions of all scribes and Pharisees. We know of at least some early Pharisaic rabbis who probably would have even agreed with what Jesus says here.

Yet Jesus calls out at least some of these powerful religious leaders: "But do not do as they do, for they do not practice what they teach," he says. "They tie up heavy burdens, hard to bear, and lay them on the shoulders of others, but they themselves are unwilling to lift a finger to move them" (23:3–4). These religious leaders insist on their followers' rigid adherence to their interpretation of the Torah, leaving no room for mercy.

Which leads to this zinger: "Woe to you, scribes and Pharisees, hypocrites! For you tithe mint, dill, and cumin and have neglected the weightier matters of the law: justice and mercy and faith. It is these you ought to have practiced without neglecting the others. You blind guides! You strain out a gnat but swallow a camel!" (23:23–24). In Jesus' way of love, pursuing justice and mercy and faith is greater than obeying the smallest details of the Law—which Jesus assumes all Jews should follow, including himself.

Here's the problem Jesus is addressing: *purity plus power easily turns into exclusion and oppression.* When those with power over others adopt a mindset of rigid separation from all they deem impure, they can use their power to control those under their power, to pronounce them unclean (whether or not they truly are), and ultimately to exclude them. And to this, God says to us through Jesus, "I desire mercy, not sacrifice."

Pursuing mercy is hard. This is much harder than simply "Don't do fake religion, kids, and throw a little love around, eh?" This is hard: paying attention to those on the fringes, showing compassion to those on the edges, welcoming to our common table those on the margins, especially those our tradition or our community has labeled "sinners."

This is a hard teaching, but walking in Jesus' footsteps, walking in his Spirit, we can do it.

"MERCY, NOT SACRIFICE": MATTHEW 12

We take that bit of homework back to Jesus our Teacher, and he turns to us yet again: "Go and learn what this means: I desire mercy, not sacrifice."

So let's turn to another time Jesus says those very same words: Matthew 12.

Here Jesus' disciples walk through a field, plucking and eating grain—on the Sabbath, the prescribed day of rest. They could have exercised a bit of self-control, a bit of patience until the next meal! And what were they doing going on a journey on the Sabbath anyway? Later, Jesus heals a man with a withered hand—on the Sabbath. The condition wasn't anything new. Surely he could have waited one more day!

The Really Religious (yep, that's still me) get on Jesus' case once again. This time, though, they're putting the letter of the Law—strict Sabbath observance, that is, sacrifice—ahead of the spirit of the Law: mercy.

As the Son of Man, the Human with a capital *H*, Jesus is Lord over the Sabbath law. The Sabbath, Jesus says, was made for humans, not humans for the Sabbath. His words suggest that the entire Law of Moses is made for humans, not humans for the Law. And so Jesus, much like some of his contemporaries in the School of Hillel, prioritizes the Torah's spirit of mercy over its rigid observance.

It can be hard for Christians to see the spirit of mercy in the Law of Moses. Many Christians have been taught that the "Old Testament God" is all about judgment, even violently so. But a spirit of mercy pervades the Torah, if we're willing to see it.

Mercy is there right at the beginning of the Law, when God declares, "I am the LORD your God, who brought you out of the land of Egypt, out of the house of slavery" (Exodus 20:2).

Mercy is there when God decrees a weekly day of Sabbath-rest, not just for the rich and powerful, but for all—even the animals (Exodus 20:8–11; 23:12).

Mercy is there when God stipulates that indebted Jewish slaves must be freed in the seventh year, released from their debt (Exodus 21:2).

Mercy is there when God limits retribution to only a comparable level of violence: "eye for eye, tooth for tooth" (Exodus 21:23–25).

Mercy is there when God orders wealthy landowners to leave the edges and corners of their harvest fields for the poor and the foreigner to gather for themselves (Leviticus 19:9–10).

Mercy is there when God requires that wealthy landowners pay their laborers daily so they can provide for their daily needs (Leviticus 19:13).

Mercy is there when God demands that the deaf and blind be treated well, with full access to all they need (Leviticus 19:14).

And mercy is there when God commands God's people to "love your neighbor as yourself" (Leviticus 19:18).

Sure, in some of these commands we might feel that a literal reading of the Torah doesn't go far enough—Jesus himself thought so about the "eye for an eye" commandment (see Matthew 5:38–39). There are other commands in the Law of Moses where it's hard to see any mercy present. But God's mercy is there—in the Law, in the Prophets, in the Writings, and on into the New Testament—if we have eyes to see it.

And this is the spirit of mercy that Jesus prioritizes in the Law over its rigid observance.

This, too, is harder to do than simply avoiding play-acting at religion and being nice to one another. It is hard work to discern the underlying spirit of biblical teaching, to look through the letter of the Bible to see what the Holy Spirit's deeper purpose is.

But when in doubt, Jesus says, we must choose mercy. Chances are good that's what the Spirit is pointing us to, for "the Lord, the Lord, [is] a God merciful and gracious, slow to anger, and abounding in steadfast love and faithfulness" (Exodus 34:6).

"MERCY, NOT SACRIFICE": JESUS' SELF-SACRIFICE

We take that bit of homework back to Jesus our Teacher, thinking that surely we must have got it all by now. But our rabbi turns to us one more time: "Go and learn what this means: I desire mercy, not sacrifice."

We shouldn't be surprised. Jesus' teachings are like this, remember? Out of the storehouses of Jesus' kingdom teachings we draw out wisdom both age-old and ever-new (Matthew 13:52). But how can there be more to this? We've looked back at Hosea 6, where God first said this. We've looked at two of the places where Jesus quotes this.

"I desire mercy, not sacrifice." What other sacrifice might Jesus mean? More than just the Law-prescribed offerings, or the right religious rituals? More than just living by the letter of the Law? What other sacrifice is there?

Oh, right.

There's Jesus himself. Jesus gave his own life as a sacrifice.

But since Jesus did this, what does it mean to say that Jesus—or God, for whom Jesus speaks—does not desire sacrifice?

How about this: *It means no sacrifice of anyone, anytime, in any way.*

Jesus' innocent self-sacrifice was an end to all sacrifice: not just animal sacrifice, not just religious offerings, but all the ways in which we sacrifice a life to gain the favor of the gods or to create favorable circumstances for ourselves.

No sacrifice, then. No daughters and sons sacrificed in war for The Nation or The Wealthy Few. No condemned prisoners sacrificed eye for eye and life for life. No brown people sacrificed over there, or right here, to maintain "peace" or satisfy "justice" or fill the White Man's endless craving for land and cotton and sugar and water and oil.

No sacrifice, ever. No women suffering abuse while the church keeps silent, all to maintain the church's (and men's) reputation and power. No children murdered in school on the altar to the twin gods Gun and Mammon. No sexual minorities scapegoated so that straight folks don't have to deal with their own sin. No mothers cast out into the wilderness bearing the burden of responsibility for their child.

No sacrifice. No sacrifice, of anyone, ever.

Only mercy. Only, and forever, mercy.

CARVING THE CROSS

Jesus sat cross-legged against the outside wall of his home, eyes focused on the work of his hands. He was carving a piece of wood, the dead branch of an olive tree he had picked up the day before. Joseph had shown him how to carve the wood, knowing when to cut against the grain and when to work with it, creating something out of nothing much.

Mary sat beside him on a stool, pitting olives into a bowl at her feet. She glanced at Jesus as she worked. He was so intense, this son of hers, as if all the meaning of the universe was held in his gaze.

Mary suddenly realized this gaze was focused on her. "Mother," Jesus asked, "Rabbi Eleazar said there haven't always been sacrifices in the temple in Jerusalem. Is that true?"

Mary was well-acquainted with Jesus' questions, coming, as they so often did, out of the blue. "Yes," she replied, "many, many years ago the temple was destroyed, and our people were taken away and lived in exile. There was no temple then, so there were no sacrifices."

Jesus tilted his head in that peculiar way of his. "But how, then, were our sins atoned for?" he asked. "How did we cleanse our impurities when we became unclean? How did we show our thanksgiving to God?"

Mary paused her work, knife in one hand, olive in the other, and turned her full attention on Jesus. "Did you ask Rabbi Eleazar these questions? He is your teacher, after all."

"Yes, Imma," Jesus replied with a nod. "He told me to ask my mother."

Mary's eyes widened at this. She didn't even know Rabbi Eleazar, not really. He was a respected rabbi who came once a week from Sepphoris. She remembered him vaguely from her days as a young girl in the city, but she had never spoken with him.

Unless . . . unless word had reached even the synagogues of Sepphoris.

"Mercy," Mary whispered. "That's the only way sin can be atoned for. It's the only way to become pure once again. It's the only way, even, to give thanks to God." She swallowed, her lips gone dry. "Mercy."

Jesus' brow furrowed as he thought about this. His gaze never left Mary, that soul-piercing gaze of his. Mary had to look away.

"What is mercy, Imma?" Jesus asked gently.

What is mercy? How to describe for this ten-year-old boy the shame she had felt at being a pregnant, unwed teen in a small village like Nazareth? Being a poor peasant girl with nothing to offer an upright and upstanding craftsman like Joseph? Being outcast by some of her own kin, and downtrodden by an uncaring world?

But then: God, speaking to her; Joseph, standing by her. All this mercy, embodied in the young boy sitting before her.

"Mercy," Mary said, the words welling up from deep in her spirit, "mercy is power turned upside down. Someone has power over you, power to condemn you, power to exclude you, power to bend you to their will—but they don't. Instead, they forgive you, they welcome you, they give you freedom. They give you power."

She looked back at Jesus, holding his gaze. "That is mercy."

Jesus nodded thoughtfully. "So mercy is greater than sacrifice?"

Mary smiled at her son. "Every time, my little Yeshu," she said. "Every time."

Jesus returned her smile and turned his gaze back to the wood in his hands. Only then did Mary notice the curious shape he was carving: a face, the face of a man, wrenched in agony, in excruciating pain. As if—Mary's breath caught—as if this man had been crucified.

SIX

David's Son
or David's Lord?

The LORD says to my lord,
"Sit at my right hand
until I make your enemies your footstool."

—PSALM 110:1

TEACHING IN THE TEMPLE

They were frantic.

Mary and Joseph had been searching for Jesus for many hours, the anxiety building for days. They had left Jerusalem after the Passover festival, heading back to Nazareth with all their kin. It was best to travel in large groups, for even Rome's vaunted peace did not extend to every highway and byway on the fringes of its empire.

At the end of the first day's travel, though, they realized Jesus was not with them. They panicked, searching every face around every fire, calling his name. They came to the horrible realization that they had left Jesus behind in Jerusalem.

Back they had gone as soon as daylight allowed, a whole day's journey again but this time more quickly done, the fears unspoken among them, driving their every step back to Jerusalem. That very evening they began searching the city, dividing up the task with uncles and aunts and anyone who would help. An alert had gone out, and no one minded the inconvenience: one day it could be their child or grandchild lost and alone and afraid.

On the third day, Jesus was found by them. Not in the first place they had looked, but not the last and most desperate of their options. They were surprised, nonetheless: there he was, revealed on the southern steps of the temple, sitting among the Teachers of Israel.

Mary would never forget the scene. Some of the greatest rabbis of all Israel were there, seated along the top step, their faces glowing in the late afternoon sun. Before them, gathered at their feet, were their best and brightest students: future rabbis, many of them. And Jesus was there among them, surely the youngest among them at twelve years old.

Mary wanted to rush to him, to shake him in anger at his care-lessness, to hold him tight in relief at his safety. But Joseph reached out a hand, stopping her. For Jesus was not merely among these rabbis and their disciples, listening to them teach and discuss and debate the Torah. Jesus himself was now speaking.

"I have heard the Psalms sung in our synagogue since I was a child," Jesus was saying. Smiles greeted this pronouncement, spoken by a child with a child's confidence. "And there is one psalm that stays forever in my mind: 'A psalm of David. The Lord says to my lord: Sit at my right hand, until I make your enemies your footstool.'"

Jesus paused, scanning the faces of the eminent teachers before him. "Can you tell me, master rabbis, who this is who is David's lord?"

"It is Abraham," replied the oldest and most venerable of the great rabbis without hesitation, "for who else had the blessing of Melchizedek? David speaks of one being ordained a priest in the order of Melchizedek, and Moses himself tells the story of our father Abraham being blessed by Melchizedek, priest of God Most High."

"But that cannot be," said another rabbi of nearly equal age and honor. "For in what sense was Abraham ordained to Melchizedek's priesthood? And in what sense was Abraham placed at God's right hand with every enemy conquered at his feet, as David's psalm describes?"

"It is the coming Messiah," pronounced another, younger rabbi, "a prophecy yet to be fulfilled. The LORD God will give the Lord Messiah all authority within God's kingdom, and all God's enemies will bow down in submission to him."

"I agree it is the Messiah," Jesus replied. Eyes widened in aston-ishment that this boy from Galilee would dare to offer his opinion among such learned company. "But how, then, does David call him 'lord'? A son is not greater than his father; no descendant is greater than her ancestor. A son of David should call David lord. Yet here King David calls his own son his lord and master." Jesus looked at each of the revered rabbis in turn. "How can this be?"

A clamor of responses arose around Jesus, the rabbis in vigorous debate, their disciples basking in their wisdom. But all Mary could see was Jesus, her beloved son, sitting among the Teachers of Israel in the House of God.

Who was he, this son of hers, this son of David, this son of God? Twelve years old, twelve years and more her son, yet as mystifying to her as the day the angel came.

WHO IS JESUS?

"The LORD said to my Lord: 'Sit at my right hand, until I put your enemies under your feet.'"

As strange as it might seem, this is the Old Testament verse that is most quoted in the New Testament. And this psalm, Psalm 110, is the most quoted Old Testament chapter in the New Testament.

In the book of Acts, the apostles describe Jesus as exalted by God in his resurrection, "sitting at God's right hand," dispensing God's forgiveness (2:33–34; 5:31).

In the letters of Paul, the resurrected Jesus "sits at God's right hand," interceding with God on behalf of believers (Romans 8:34) and exercising God's power and authority (Ephesians 1:20).

In the anonymous letter to the Hebrews, Jesus sits "at the right hand of the Majesty on high," a position not even the angels can aspire to (1:3, 13), where Jesus mediates our relationship with God as our high priest (8:1).

In 1 Peter, the resurrected Jesus "has gone into heaven and is at the right hand of God, with angels, authorities, and powers made subject to him" (3:22).

This was an important text of Scripture for the apostles and the first Christians, perhaps in part because it was such an important text of Scripture for Jesus. What was it about this verse, even this psalm, that Jesus and his first followers saw as so significant? And what might that mean for us today?

To read the Bible with Jesus, we've been looking at some of his favorite passages in his Scriptures, the Jewish Scriptures, which form the Christian Old Testament. So far, all these favorite scripture passages of Jesus have given us a strong sense of the gospel Jesus preached, the message Jesus taught, and the way Jesus lived his life. In this chapter and the next, we'll consider Bible favorites of Jesus that give us a strong sense of who Jesus was and who he still is for us today.

JESUS IS THE CHRIST

There's an interesting fact about the gospel of Mark: in Mark's gospel, Jesus never calls himself the Messiah, or the Christ. Not only that—throughout the gospel, if anyone does dare call him the Messiah, Jesus commands them to silence.

Scholars call this the "messianic secret." This messianic secret is found in Matthew and Luke as well, and in a different way in John, but it's most pronounced in Mark, the earliest of the Gospels written. Mark's reluctance to name Jesus as the Messiah has raised the question: Did Jesus himself truly believe he was the Messiah, or was this a later invention of the early Christians?

It's a fascinating debate—and our text from Mark's gospel is on the front lines of it. My own view is that Jesus indeed came to view himself as the Messiah, but not in the way that people of his day—or even our own, for that matter—understood this.

Let's start with a common misunderstanding we have today: the word "Messiah" does not mean "divine." No one in Jesus' day believed the Messiah was the LORD, the one Creator in whom all things exist, and nowhere in the New Testament does the title "Messiah" or "Christ" in itself suggest divinity. Rather, "Messiah" (from Hebrew) or "Christ" (from Greek) means "anointed one," and it refers to the ancient practice of ritually anointing someone with oil for a sacred task: a priest, a prophet, or a king.

In the New Testament, to say that Jesus is the Messiah is to say that Jesus is the human descendant of the ancient Israelite King David who brings about God's reign on earth—the "kingdom of God." "Messiah," or "Christ," therefore, in the New Testament essentially means "King."

Not everyone in Jesus' day would have agreed with this understanding of a coming Messiah. Some Jews looked for two Messiahs—one a priest, the other a king—while other Jews didn't expect a Messiah at all. But a common understanding in that day was that there would be a Messiah, and that when he came he would overthrow Israel's enemies by military conquest (including and especially the Romans). Then he would reestablish God's reign as it was in the glory days of David and Solomon, ruling from his throne in Jerusalem.

Needless to say, Jesus didn't do this.

There's a telling moment in Mark's gospel when Peter confesses that Jesus is the Messiah (Mark 8:27–33). Jesus tells the disciples not to say anything about this to anyone—that whole messianic secret thing. But then Jesus describes how he must go to Jerusalem and be rejected, and be killed, and after three days rise again.

This was not Peter's vision of the Messiah! Peter's vision of the Messiah was apparently the commonly held view that the Messiah would raise an army and march on Jerusalem and rid the land of the Romans. *Not* that the Messiah would lead a rabble of pilgrim peasants to Jerusalem to die at the hands of the Romans.

So Peter takes Jesus aside and rebukes him. In response, Jesus turns to Peter and rebukes *him*: "Get behind me, Satan! You are not thinking in God's ways, but in human ways."

That way of bringing about God's reign on earth—through violence and coercion and worldly power—is not God's way of doing so.

It's a theme we see throughout the Gospels.

The devil offers Jesus all "the kingdoms of the world"— absolute political power—and Jesus rejects him with words almost identical to his rebuke of Peter: "Away with you, Satan!" (Matthew 4:8–10).

The crowds are fed by Jesus with a few loaves of bread and a couple of fish, and so they try to "take him by force to make him king" (imagine, he could feed an army!). But Jesus sees their intention and escapes from them "to the mountain by himself" (John 6:14–15).

In the garden of Gethsemane, as Judas and the soldiers approach to take Jesus away for trial, Jesus has one last opportunity to save himself from suffering, to choose the way of power instead of weakness, the way of glory instead of the way of the cross. He rejects this worldly way with that famous prayer to God: "Yet not my will but yours be done" (Luke 22:42).

Pontius Pilate, the Roman governor of Judea, an expert at maintaining the "kingdom" of Rome through violence, can't make sense of this so-called "King" Jesus standing before him. Especially when Jesus denounces the ways of violence and says to him, "My kingdom is not of this world" (John 18:33–36).

This, I believe, is what's behind Mark's messianic secret. People, then and now, want a Messiah who will use the world's power to their own advantage, even if it disadvantages others. People want a Messiah who will deal decisively with "those people" while lifting up and centering "our people." People want a Messiah who is willing to coerce others, even to use violence against them, if necessary.

Jesus is the Messiah. But he's not that kind of Messiah.

And so he forbade people from calling him "Messiah."

JESUS CHRIST IS LORD

But Psalm 110 points to that kind of Messiah, doesn't it? The military Messiah, the conquering Christ?

It speaks of "enemies" being made a "footstool": the image is of a victorious warlord seated at the right hand of the king, his feet on the neck of his conquered enemies lying prostrate before him. It speaks of "kings" being "shattered" on the "day of [the Lord Messiah's] wrath." It speaks of corpses filling the earth in this Lord Messiah's judgment.

That sure doesn't sound like Jesus' kind of Messiah. This is not Jesus the Messiah teaching love of enemies and praying forgiveness for his crucifiers from the cross! How did this psalm become such a favorite of Jesus and his apostles?

Jesus, like John the Baptist before him and most of the first Christians after him, swam in a stream of Jewish thinking called "apocalyptic." In apocalyptic thinking, human history is moving toward a world-overturning event: God will arrive on the scene, bringing judgment upon God's enemies and deliverance for God's people. For many early Jews in this stream of thought, this meant that God's Messiah would come, God's martyred people would be raised from the dead, and God's eternal reign would begin.

Here's the thing: in this apocalyptic way of thinking, human beings are not our ultimate enemies. Rather, when we pull aside the veil of the way things seem to be—when we experience a "revelation" of how things truly are (which is what "apocalypse" means)—we find fouler things at work in the deep places of our world. Behind the unjust and evil oppressors of this world, invisible forces are at play. Behind all this world's Pharaohs and Caesars and Führers and more, there are unseen powers that seem to control us but which we can never seem to control.

These are spiritual forces. This means they are not human, not mere flesh and blood, however much they work in and through individual people and groups. They are not even necessarily personal forces, though most Jews in Jesus' day believed that they were. An invisible, malevolent, personal being is not lurking behind every act of evil. But these spiritual forces are real, nonetheless.[1]

Think of what happens when a crowd becomes a mob. A crowd is simply a bunch of people in the same place at the same time. A mob, though, is a crowd compelled by more primitive, animal instincts, animated by a spirit of fear, perhaps, or overcome by a spirit of violence.

Or think about what happens when an ordinary person attains a position of power. Access to power over others, the power to do whatever one wants in the world, can change a person profoundly—as if the person is inhabited by a different temperament, a different spirit, than they were before.

People will do things as a mob that they would never do as individuals. People will do things when they have power that they would never do without that power. This—individuals driven by a spirit of power and mobs driven by a spirit of fear and violence—is how Jesus got crucified.

All this is what Christians call "sin": our malicious fears, our willful ignorance, our stubborn pride, our selfishness, greed, lust, hatred, disgust, cruelty, violence, rage, and more. And this sin results in death: everything from disabling shame and incapacitating guilt to broken relationships, intense suffering, and yes, physical death. Read the origins story of Genesis 3—all this is the curse of "death" that comes about from the disobedience of the first humans.

This Sin with a capital *S* and Death with a capital *D* are our true enemies. Not one another, not any human being or human group.

The powers of Sin and Death at work in us and among us can become baked right into the structures and systems of our societies—our political systems, our economic systems, our social structures. Individual fears and ignorance of the different "other," spurred by disgust and morphed into cruelty, become racism—and collectively show themselves in inequitable voting maps and discriminatory government programs. Individual greed, driven by pride and a lust for power, leads to the accumulation of vast wealth by the few—and collectively leads to rampant poverty and ecological catastrophe.

"Our struggle," Ephesians 6 reminds us, "is not against blood and flesh but against the rulers, against the authorities, against the cosmic powers of this present darkness, against the spiritual forces of evil" (6:12). And we resist these evil powers through pursuing truth, justice, peace, and faith, wielding the good news of Jesus and praying always in the Spirit (6:13–18).

We resist these evil powers, that is, by loving our neighbors as ourselves—including our human enemies.

This is not how all those swimming in the stream of early Jewish apocalyptic understood things. Some, while seeing spiritual powers behind the human rulers, structures, and systems of this world, expected that God would violently destroy God's enemies—both the spiritual and the human ones. Some of them expected to participate in this violent judgment of their human enemies. But the early Christians, consistently over the first three centuries, followed Jesus in his way of nonviolent resistance of evil powers, loving their flesh-and-blood enemies the same as their neighbors.

This, then, is how the first followers of Jesus understood Psalm 110. Jesus of Nazareth, the Son of David who brings about God's reign on earth, has been exalted by God as Lord, raised up from the dead to God's right hand, and given all authority in heaven and earth. He will reign relentlessly until all God's true enemies—all these deeper powers at work in us and among us—are brought into submission to his rule of love.

In other words, Jesus Christ is Lord.

Jesus Christ is Lord—not prime ministers or presidents, not the wealthy one percent or the up-and-coming movers and shakers, not your boss or your teacher or your spouse or your parent, not me, not you.

Jesus Christ is Lord—Lord over all injustice and oppression, all structural inequities and systemic racism, all greedy corporations and climate-changing polluters, and all our own leanings toward selfishness and pride.

Jesus Christ is Lord—Lord in your sickness and in your health, Lord in your poverty and over your wealth, Lord in your failures and in your successes, Lord in your strength and especially through your weakness.

Jesus Christ is Lord—Lord over your life, your relationships, your family, your home life and work life and church life, all your comings and goings and waking ups and lying downs.

Jesus Christ is Lord—and he commands our allegiance, to follow him in his way of love even if it means disappointing our families and friends and defying the powers that be in our world.

Jesus Christ is Lord—and he reigns in love.

Jesus Christ is Lord—and he reigns in love.

Jesus Christ is Lord—and he reigns, always and forever, in love.

SEVEN

The Coming Son of Man

As I watched in the night visions,
I saw one like a human being [a son of man]
   coming with the clouds of heaven.
And he came to the Ancient One
   and was presented before him.
To him was given dominion
   and glory and kingship,
that all peoples, nations, and languages
   should serve him.
His dominion is an everlasting dominion
   that shall not pass away,
and his kingship is one
   that shall never be destroyed.

—DANIEL 7:13–14

JESUS THE "SON OF MAN"

We have come a long way in a short while in our reading of the Bible with Jesus.

We've looked at what Jesus called the greatest commandment—devoted love for God—based on the Shema recited every morning and evening by every devout Jew, Deuteronomy 6:4–9.

We've looked at how Jesus extended this Shema by combining it with the "love of neighbor" command in Leviticus 19:18: we are to love God in undivided devotion primarily by loving others with unwavering, generous compassion.

We've looked at Jesus' mission statement from Isaiah 61:1–2: God has called Jesus—and through Jesus, his followers—to bring the good news of God's Jubilee to the world, God's reign of justice and peace and life for all, but especially for the most vulnerable and disadvantaged.

We've looked at the difficult teaching of Jesus based on Isaiah 6:9–10, that many people will refuse to open their hearts up to his teaching of transformative love—self-giving, other-welcoming, justice-bringing, kingdom-building love. But those who do will find abundant life, enough for all.

We've looked at Jesus' challenging reference to Hosea 6:6, the homework he gives us, like an end-of-term project, to "go and learn what this means," that God desires "mercy and not sacrifice." Mercy trumps law-abiding sacrifice, every time.

And we've looked at Jesus' enigmatic use of Psalm 110:1, that the Messiah is David's Lord and not merely his descendant,

ruling at God's right hand until all God's ultimate enemies—Sin and its resulting Death—are conquered.

In this chapter I want to explore something that is found
throughout Jesus' teaching in the Gospels yet is something we
don't often give much thought to.

Earlier, I mentioned that Jesus never directly calls himself
"Messiah" in the Gospels. There is, however, a title that Jesus
does use for himself. It's a phrase many of us don't give a second
glance to because we're so used to it, even though it's a little
strange when you stop and think about it.

Jesus calls himself "the Son of Man." And he does this a lot.
About eighty times in the Gospels, in fact.

> "Foxes have holes, and birds of the air have nests, but the
> Son of Man has nowhere to lay his head" (Matthew 8:20).

> "The Son of Man has authority on earth to forgive sins" (9:6).

> "The Son of Man came eating and drinking, and they say,
> 'Look, a glutton and a drunkard, a friend of tax collectors
> and sinners!' Yet wisdom is vindicated by her deeds" (11:19).

> "The Son of Man is lord of the Sabbath" (12:8).

> "Truly I tell you, there are some standing here who will not
> taste death before they see the Son of Man coming in his
> kingdom" (16:28).

> "The Son of Man is going to be betrayed into human hands,
> and they will kill him, and on the third day he will be raised"
> (17:22–23).

> "The Son of Man came not to be served but to serve and to
> give his life a ransom for many" (20:28).

"When the Son of Man comes in his glory and all the angels with him, then he will sit on the throne of his glory" (25:31).

"From now on you will see the Son of Man seated at the right hand of Power and coming on the clouds of heaven" (26:64).

And that's only a sample, just from the gospel of Matthew. It's all throughout the Gospels, Jesus calling himself the Son of Man. What's up with that?

JESUS THE EARTHLY SON OF MAN

Imagine if I went around saying, "Michael is doing this . . ." or "Michael believes that . . ." People would think I was a little odd. Perhaps if I were rich or a celebrity they'd think I was merely eccentric. Either way, it's strange for people to refer to themselves in the third person.

But imagine if I not only referred to myself in the third person but referred to myself with a title: "The White Guy is doing this . . ." or "The White Guy thinks that . . ." I'd have to be *really* rich or famous to get away with that level of oddity!

Well, it would have been just as odd in Jesus' day for someone to go around referring to themselves as the Son of Man. Jesus wasn't rich, and he wasn't especially famous, so he couldn't get away with being eccentric. But he did it anyway, and for a particular reason: it highlighted something important about how Jesus understood himself.

Even though it was likely odd to others that Jesus referred to himself as "the Son of Man," the phrase itself, "son of man," was a perfectly ordinary phrase in Jesus' day. It simply meant "a human being" or, more generally, "humankind."

Think of Psalm 8, for example. Psalm 8:4 says, "What are humans that you are mindful of them, mortals [literally, the son of man] that you care for them?" The phrase "the son of man" is a way of referring to humankind in all our mortal frailty and finiteness. Or take a glance through the book of Ezekiel. You'll find the phrase "son of man" used repeatedly throughout. It's God's way of referring to Ezekiel—"O son of man," meaning "O mortal"—in contrast to God's divinity and immortality.

So when Jesus calls himself the Son of Man, he is emphasizing his full humanity, his true humanity. He's not some transcendent divine being, floating along as he walked, untouched by the dust of earth. He is *of* the dust of the earth, formed like the first human from the very earth itself, just like every other human being who has ever lived.

But of course human beings have never merely been "of the dust of the earth." As the creation story in Genesis 2 puts it, we're also breathed into by the breath of God (2:7). We may be crafted from carbon and steeped in water, evolved from a single-celled organism billions of years ago, but like all other living creatures, we've also got the very life of God within us (Psalm 104:29–30).

Genesis 1:26–27 underscores this in even stronger terms, stating that humankind—and every human being—has been made "in God's image." Being created in God's image means that we are given a particular responsibility: as humans we are called to represent God on earth, to extend God's reign of love and light and life to all creation. That's what the language of "dominion" in Genesis 1 and "tending the earth" in Genesis 2 is all about.

That's also precisely where Psalm 8 goes. Here's the wider context of the psalm:

When I look at your heavens, the work of your fingers,
        the moon and the stars that you have established;
what are humans that you are mindful of them,
        mortals [the son of man] that you care for them?
Yet you have made them a little lower than God,
        and crowned them with glory and honor.
You have given them dominion over the works of your
        hands. (vv. 3–6)

We are all sons of Adam, daughters of Eve,[1] children of
Humanity, made of dust and water. Yet we're all created in
God's image, crowned with divine glory and honor, made to be
God's representatives on earth, extending God's dominion of
faithful love throughout creation.

Many times when Jesus uses the phrase "Son of Man," these
are therefore the kinds of things he is thinking of: he is the
"Human One," representing the full promise and responsibility
of humanity. When he heals on the Sabbath, for example, he says,
"The Sabbath was made for humankind and not humankind for
the Sabbath, so the Son of Man"—Jesus, that is, representing all
humankind—"is lord even of the Sabbath" (Mark 2:27–28).

JESUS THE EXALTED SON OF MAN

But there's still more to all this. There are a few times when
Jesus uses Son of Man to refer to a specific passage from his
Scriptures, one that puts an extra strong spin on all this:
Daniel 7. This was a popular passage of Scripture in some cir-
cles in Jesus' day—and part of the basis for that apocalyptic
stream of Judaism we were introduced to last chapter.

Daniel 7 describes a dream, a prophetic vision, Daniel had.
In the dream he sees four beasts, each one more monstrous than

the one before. A lion with eagles' wings. A bear with three tusks coming out of its mouth. A leopard with four wings and four heads. And a fourth beast unidentifiable as an animal, but "terrifying and dreadful and exceedingly strong" (v. 7), with iron teeth and ten horns. These beasts, we're told, represent four successive "kings" or empires in human history: perhaps the ancient Babylonian Empire, then the Persian Empire, then the Greeks, and the Seleucids.

Then, in sharp contrast to these horrific, horrible beasts, these inhuman empires, these oppressive powers of this age, "one like a son of man" comes "with the clouds of heaven" into the throne room of God, and God gives this son of man "dominion" over all the earth (vv. 13–14). In other words, this is a kingdom with a human face, a human touch, a humane realm: this is the kingdom of God. In *other*, other words, this is humanity fulfilling its original divine purpose: extending God's reign of love and light and life to all creation.

Jesus is Daniel's Son of Man. Representing all humanity, realizing our potential as humans created in God's image, Jesus receives God's dominion and exercises it, accomplishing all God's good intentions for humanity and all creation.

The upshot of all Jesus' strange references to himself as Son of Man in the Gospels?

Jesus comes as Son of Man, fully and truly human, sharing in our humanity. As Son of Man, Jesus shares all our weakness, all our frailty, all the dust and dirt of our bodily existence.

Jesus comes as Son of Man, representing us as humankind. As Son of Man, Jesus draws us up into God's presence, paving the way for us to fulfill God's purpose for us created in God's image.

Jesus comes as Son of Man to receive God's eternal dominion and to reign over all the earth in love and light and life,
in contrast to all the monstrous, inhuman empires and evil
powers that continue to plague our world.

And in Jesus' birth and life, his baptism and transfiguration,
his healing and teaching, at the cross and in the resurrection
and at the renewal of all things, all this is fulfilled. Jesus is
this coming Son of Man.

TO THE RIVER

The dust caked his feet and coated his sandals. His throat was
parched, aching with thirst. The sweat dripped down his back
beneath his tunic. He wiped his brow with the back of his dirt-
grimed hand. He thought of his destination, the cool River
Jordan, and pressed forward on the rocky path.

It is time for the Son of Man to be revealed.

The words echoed in his mind. They were his mother's enigmatic words, spoken over him just a few days ago, when Jesus
had said goodbye to her. He was no longer a child, or even a
young man. He was a carpenter of Nazareth, a rabbi of Galilee.
But he was still his mother's son.

It is time for the Son of Man to be revealed.

Each downhill step brought him closer to his destination, the
beginning of a new journey. He felt each step in his bones. He
felt the burning in his thighs, the quickening of his breath. He
felt the weight of his humanity upon him.

It is time for the Son of Man to be revealed.

Jesus wasn't sure entirely what Mary had meant by this, but
he knew it to be true. The Son of Man—well, we were all sons
of Adam, he thought, all daughters of Eve. But the Son of Man?
Daniel's Son of Man? Taking up all the hopes and fears of Israel?

Taking a stand against powerful empires like Rome? "Coming on the clouds of heaven"?

It is time for the Son of Man to be revealed.

He looked up, sunward, shielding his eyes. No clouds to ride today, he smiled grimly to himself. No rain on the horizon. Just the relentless heat, the endless dust, the narrow path ahead of him, leading to a muddy river now visible in the distance. The river the people of Israel crossed into the Promised Land. The river that Naaman the Gentile bathed in to be healed.

It is time for the Son of Man to be revealed.

He did know what this meant. It meant God's vision for the world was about to be planted in the soil of this very earth: true justice, lasting peace, abundant life for all humanity, even all creation. It meant his own humanity tested to its limits, to its limits and probably beyond.

It is time for the Son of Man to be revealed.

He whispered the words to himself as he walked through the gathered crowd on the river's edge. He whispered the words to himself as he stepped into the water, moving to John's side. He whispered the words to himself as he nodded at John's questioning look, as he went under the water supported by John's rough yet gentle hands.

It is time for the Son of Man to be revealed.

As he came up, the words echoed back to him in the depths of his soul: "You are my Son." He saw the cloudless heavens torn asunder by a near-blinding light, and a cool breeze blew upon him as gentle as a dove, like the very breath of God. "You are my beloved Son, and I am well pleased with you."

And with those words reverberating within him, beating to the rhythm of his pounding heart, Jesus set his face toward the wilderness.

Continuing to Read the Bible with Jesus

I HOPE YOU'VE learned something with me as we've read the Bible with Jesus. And there's so much more to learn as we keep following Jesus our Rabbi, our Messiah, our Lord.

As we continue reading the Bible with Jesus, it's important to note that the Christian Bible—our Scriptures as Christians—extends beyond what Jesus knew as his Scriptures, our Old Testament. We have focused on how Jesus read his Bible, yet the things we've learned apply equally well to the New Testament as well as the Old.

I'd like to suggest three broad themes that have surfaced in our journey with Jesus so far. These thoughts can provide a guide for us as we continue to read the Bible with Jesus.

First, *we must allow Scripture to permeate our lives.*

It's ironic: Jesus never had his own NIV Student Bible, marked up and taped up and carried around in a zippered Bible cover—yet he was surrounded by the words of his Scriptures from morning to evening every day from birth to death. He had not just memorized Scripture, he had internalized it.

The Shema with its command to love God with everything we are. The oracles of Isaiah with their declarations of the good news of God's Jubilee reign. The Psalms with their songs of praise and gratitude and deepest lament.

How can we allow Scripture to permeate our lives like Jesus did?

It might mean doing something Jesus could never do—reading the Bible regularly on our own.

It might mean doing something Jesus did often—memorizing large portions of scripture.

It might mean reciting the "Jesus Creed" morning and evening—the extended Shema described in chapter 2.

It might mean gathering regularly in a small group to read and study Scripture.

It might mean allowing greater time for the simple yet impassioned reading of Scripture in our worship services.

It might mean listening to an audio Bible, or learning, listening, and singing songs and hymns based on biblical texts.

Of course, we know that simply reading the Bible is not enough. Simply knowing what's in the Bible is not enough. We do need to soak ourselves in Scripture, like Jesus did, but we also need to hear it and read it in a particular way, like Jesus did.

Second, then, *we need to pay attention to what's "heavier" and what's "lighter" in Scripture.*

We've learned from Jesus what this means.

It means giving the greatest weight in Scripture to two commandments from the Torah: love of God, and love of neighbor, or even, loving God by loving others. This is the sum of all our obligations before God.

It means weighing mercy as greater than sacrifice, showing mercy toward others as greater than rigid Bible-obedience, greater than doing prescribed biblical practices, greater than keeping ourselves separate from things or people we deem impure.

It means viewing this love and mercy as "the spirit of the law" behind "the letter of the law": finding the merciful motivation behind laws and commands, highlighting the threads of love through Scripture, reading the difficult passages in light of these themes of love and mercy.

It means, therefore, reading the Bible through the lens of love. Put in the negative, if we come up with an interpretation of a passage in the Bible that leads us to *not* love another person in the way Jesus loves us—open-handed, with open arms—we are not reading the Bible rightly. Positively, when we read the Bible with Jesus, we learn to love God by loving others: neighbors, strangers, those who are different from us, even our enemies.

When we pay attention to these weightier matters of Scripture—viewing the lighter matters through the lens of the weightier, not allowing the lighter matters of Scripture to take the place of justice-bringing love and power-sharing mercy—then we are well on our way to becoming more faithful followers of Jesus.

Which leads to a third thought: *we need to read the Bible to follow Jesus.*

We don't read the Bible to become more biblical; we read the Bible to become more Christlike.

We don't read the Bible so that we might obey a book; we read the Bible so that we might obey Jesus, our Lord.

We don't read the Bible in order to follow the Bible; we read the Bible in order to follow Jesus.

And this means, in particular, reading the Bible to follow Jesus in his way of love.

Reading the Bible to follow Jesus in devotion to God our Creator, loving God with every dimension of our being—in our pursuit of truth and holiness and experience of God, yes, but first and foremost in our love for others.

Reading the Bible, then, to follow Jesus in open-handed, open-armed love for our neighbors, including strangers and even enemies, loving them as ourselves, prioritizing their needs as if these needs were our own.

Reading the Bible to follow Jesus in expanding this love of neighbor to include the pursuit of justice—including economic justice and social justice—walking in solidarity with those who are most often unjustly treated, those without power in our world.

Reading the Bible to follow Jesus in tending to the soil of our own hearts so that we are able and willing to appreciate God's good news, to walk in Jesus' way, and to remove the obstacles that get in the way of living out Jesus' way of love.

Reading the Bible to follow Jesus in leading with mercy toward others, putting their well-being ahead of our desire to be "biblical" or even "Christian," and refusing to sacrifice their wellbeing for our own good.

Reading the Bible to follow Jesus as Lord, walking in allegiance to him and his way of love above all other people and all other ways that might claim our allegiance.

And so reading the Bible to become more fully human, fulfilling the promise for which God has created us as "children of humanity," formed of the earth, kin to all creation, created in God's image to extend God's dominion of light and love and life throughout the world.

Amen. May this be so.

Digging Deeper

THIS BOOK PRESENTS Jesus and his Scriptures in historical context, even venturing to include some historical fiction
vignettes of Jesus as a child. (By the way, this kind of "Gospels
fan fiction" has a long history. Just over a century after Jesus,
newly written gospels told apocryphal stories of Jesus, including of his childhood. Probably the most notorious of these are
the second-century writings known as the Infancy Gospel of
Thomas and the Gospel of Thomas.[1])

For readers who are curious to learn more about the historical context of Jesus and the Gospels, this section offers an
overview of four main topics, with a few resources for further
reading for each. First, though, some general historical notes.

When I say "first century" here and throughout this book, I
mean the first century CE (the Common Era, which historians
prefer to AD, or *anno Domini*, Latin for "year of our Lord").
Jesus lived in the first thirty years of the Common Era, in the
first third of the first century CE. That places him two thousand years before the present day.

To help you further situate Jesus in his own Jewish history:

King David, whether historical or in legend, lived roughly
1,000 years before Jesus, or about 1000 BCE (before the

Common Era). He was viewed as Israel's greatest king, and became the template for expectations of a royal Messiah.

The kingdoms of Israel and Judah had both fallen to foreign empires by about 600 years before Jesus: Israel to Assyria in 722 BCE, and Judah to Babylonia in 586 BCE. (Note that years BCE count down to 1; years CE count upward from 1.) Original Isaiah prophesied around 700 years before Jesus, second Isaiah perhaps 500 years before Jesus.

The Jerusalem temple was rebuilt roughly 525 years before Jesus. During this time most Jews were scattered from Babylon and Persia (the location of present-day Iraq and Iran) to Egypt. The Torah was edited and finalized over the following two or three centuries. The Psalms were collected during this time.

Alexander the Great claimed the region for the Hellenistic (Greek) Empire about 325 years before Jesus. Greek language and culture came to dominate throughout the eastern Mediterranean. Synagogues emerged in Egypt, then spread to Judea and Galilee.

There were several decades of relative Jewish independence over the region under the Hasmoneans (the family of Judas Maccabee), roughly 140 to 60 years before Jesus. The Maccabean revolt that reclaimed the temple became a celebrated event among Jews (commemorated at Hanukkah), stoking the fires of Jewish nationalism.

The Romans conquered the region about 60 years before Jesus' birth (63 BCE). Augustus was Roman emperor at Jesus' birth, Tiberias the emperor during Jesus' public ministry. The Herodian kings ruled Galilee on behalf of the Roman Empire: Herod the Great at Jesus' birth, and his son Herod Antipas at Jesus' crucifixion. Pontius Pilate served as Rome's governor in Judea at this time.

JEWISH LIFE AND COMMUNITY IN FIRST-CENTURY GALILEE

Most of Jesus' life was lived in an area maybe twenty miles by twenty miles. That's the hill country of lower Galilee and along the western shores of the Sea of Galilee. It's an area slightly larger than Calgary or Memphis, somewhat smaller than New York or Los Angeles—though first-century Galilee was very different from modern city life.

Jewish life in Galilee was primarily village life in communities of a few dozen to a few hundred people. One ancient count lists over two hundred villages in Galilee in Jesus' day (see the map, p. 126, for some of them, using their most common biblical or modern names).

While there were many devout Jews in the cities of Galilee, these cities felt much more Greek or Roman, with a higher percentage of Gentiles (non-Jews). It's no coincidence that the Gospels don't mention Jesus visiting the major Galilean cities of Tiberias and Sepphoris. It was in the villages where the Galilean Jewish heart beat most freely.

Village life in first-century Galilee was family life. It was large extended families, often with roots in the village going back generations. These families would certainly have connected through marriage to people of other villages. John's portrayal of Jesus attending a wedding in Cana (John 2:1–11), or the piece of fan fiction I've written in chapter 1, would have been a common reality in first-century Galilee.

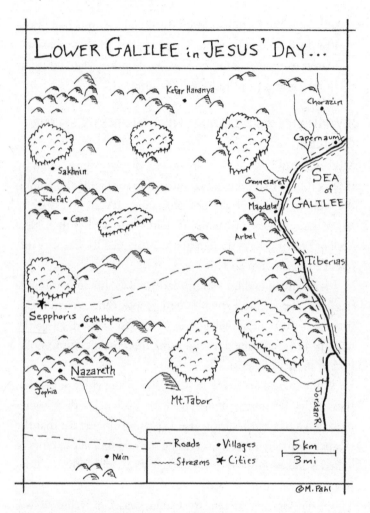

Religion permeated all of life for these Galilean Jews—and this was certainly the case for Jesus, himself a devout Jew from birth to death.

Archaeologists use three questions to determine whether a first-century village was inhabited by devout Jews: Is there evidence of immersion baths (*mikva'ot*) and stone jars? Are there tombs storing bones in ossuaries (stone boxes)? And are there any pig bones? If the answer to the first two is yes and the answer to the last is no, you've got a Jewish village. This is the case for the villages that have been excavated in Galilee.

Immersion baths and stone jars were used by first-century Jews for religious purification rituals. The practice of storing bones in ossuaries reflects the popular Jewish belief in a future resurrection of the body. Like Ezekiel's vision of dry bones (Ezekiel 37:1–14), they believed the bones are all God needs to knit the new body together. And according to the Law of Moses, pork was not kosher, or religiously clean (Leviticus 11:7–8). No pig bones? Jewish—because Gentiles loved their pork.

These features suggest that Galilean Jews were devout in all the other ways Jews throughout the Roman Empire were devout. They sought to live according to the Torah, the Law of Moses. They recited the Shema evening and morning. They followed ritual practices like eating kosher food and washing themselves to maintain religious purity. They observed the weekly Sabbath from Friday sundown to Saturday sundown, refraining from work and worshiping together in the synagogue. They circumcised their male children. And they attended major festivals in Jerusalem as they were able, offering animal sacrifices in the temple.

Synagogues were important places for worship, learning, and simply gathering within each community. There have been very few first-century synagogues uncovered in Galilee, but there's no reason to suppose that the Gospels' depiction of synagogues scattered throughout Galilee is incorrect. It's likely that synagogues in smaller villages would have been humble structures that simply haven't stood the test of time. The smallest villages might even have merely gathered in the largest home, or outdoors if the weather was good.

If you were to travel back in time to a first-century Galilean village synagogue on the Sabbath for worship, what would you find? It's hard to say for sure, but you could experience something like this.

As you approach the synagogue, you might see people washing themselves in the *mikvah* at the synagogue entrance, ritually purifying themselves to worship God and hear the Torah. As you enter, you might see a bench around the outside of the main hall; this is for the elders to sit, while others sit on the floor, perhaps on woven mats brought for this purpose. Men and women might well be sitting separately—that was later practice, but it's not clear whether that applied to first-century Galilee.

The service might open with reciting the Shema. One of the men reads from the Torah in Hebrew, another gives an Aramaic translation and provides some teaching about the text. You might also hear a reading from the Prophets with accompanying translation and instruction. Perhaps you sing some well-known psalms. There would be prayers said and a blessing pronounced. And after the service, you could well be invited to stay for a potluck—shared meals were likely a regular feature in these small-village synagogues.

Life in rural Galilee was based around subsistence farming: catching the fish, growing the crops, and tending the livestock that everyone in the family and village needed to live. In the rocky hills where Nazareth was located, people cultivated olive trees and kept small flocks of sheep and goats. The slopes to the south of Nazareth were ideal for growing grapes. On the lower slopes and in the valleys, where soil was more fertile, crops such as wheat, barley, and millet were sown. Around the Sea of Galilee, fishing was the key focus.

Goods and services would have been traded within each village and between them. Larger towns and cities would have relied on local markets for their basic necessities, with goods brought in from the surrounding farms and villages.

However, during the time of Jesus, under the rule of the Kings Herod, things began to change. Sepphoris and Tiberias were built up as significant cities. This put pressure on the surrounding towns, villages, and farms to support their growing population.

Short-term taxes were levied at times to pay for civic building programs. Farming practices were changed to increase yields to feed these growing cities. One unfortunate result: some families were forced to sell their land, often leasing back the land to farm it on the landowner's behalf, or even giving up their land entirely and becoming day laborers.

This illustrates the economic hardship faced by many rural Jews in Galilee. The Gospels often describe the working poor in Galilee, with a chain of debt around their necks and the threat of forced servitude or debtor's prison if they were unable to pay (for instance, see Matthew 18:23–35; Luke 6:20–25).

This economic hardship was brought on in part by wealthy landowners, whether Jews or non-Jews, exploiting small-scale farmers and laborers. Various layers of taxation also contributed to this hardship: short-term taxes for building projects as well as Roman land taxes on property, head taxes on every eligible individual, and tolls for trading goods across regions were added on top of the annual Jewish tax for the upkeep of the temple in Jerusalem. My fictional Ananias bar Matthias in chapter 3, while reflecting an extreme perspective, represents a harsh reality for many in first-century Galilee.

Although Jesus lived and moved in the Jewish towns and villages of Galilee, there were significant cities with a large Roman (or other non-Jewish) presence. As noted, in the region Jesus inhabited, Sepphoris and Tiberias were the main cities, each with around ten thousand inhabitants, with paved streets and smooth stone buildings and large, beautifully adorned homes where the upper crust lived.

Sepphoris, "the ornament of the Galilee," was just over an hour's walk from Nazareth. Although the Gospels never describe Jesus going there, it's reasonable to suppose he did, at least in his many years in Nazareth before he began his public ministry. There was a building boom in Sepphoris during Jesus' growing-up years as I mention in chapter 4, and it's at least possible that Joseph, a skilled artisan working with wood and stone (a *tektōn*, Matthew 13:55), found work there. Mary is also traditionally believed to have been born in Sepphoris.

The up-and-coming city in the area, however, was Tiberias, on the western shore of the Sea of Galilee. Herod Antipas, son of Herod the Great, founded the city during Jesus' life-time, and it quickly became a second center of the Herodian kingdom. However, some Jews refused to live there—it was deemed ritually impure because it was built atop a cemetery. Herod created special incentives, offering free houses and temporary exemptions from taxes, to entice people to move to the city.

Even though Jerusalem was not in Galilee but in Judea to the south, the holy city and its temple were extremely im-portant for Galilean Jews—and indeed for all Jews across the Roman Empire and beyond it. At the temple, daily sacrifices were offered on behalf of the people and annual sacrifices were made on the Day of Atonement. The temple was the center of most major festivals, including Passover. Most able-bodied Jews in Galilee would have made at least one annual pilgrimage to Jerusalem, often for Passover, where they would offer sacrifices for their sins committed and impurities accumulated over the past year.

If the synagogues were the center of worship, learning, and gathering in each community, the temple was the center of Jewish worship, learning, and gathering for all Jews around the world. Sacrifices, songs, and prayers were lifted up to God daily from dawn to dusk. People gathered in the temple courts for meetings of all kinds. And rabbis of all sorts—whether lay Pharisees, priests, scribes, or other "teachers of the Law"—taught in the temple's vast courts, in its covered porticoes, or even on the southern steps at the main entrance to the temple.

For further reading:

Stephen K. Catto, *Reconstructing the First-Century Synagogue: A Critical Analysis of Current Research* (T&T Clark, 2007).

Mark A. Chancey, *The Myth of a Gentile Galilee* (Cambridge University Press, 2002).

Craig A. Evans and Stanley E. Porter Jr., eds., *Dictionary of New Testament Background* (InterVarsity Press, 2000).

Seán Freyne, *Galilee from Alexander the Great to Hadrian, 323 BCE to 135 CE: A Study of Second Temple Judaism* (Michael Glazier and University of Notre Dame Press, 1980).

Seán Freyne, *The Jesus Movement and Its Expansion: Meaning and Mission* (Eerdmans, 2014).

Joel B. Green, Jeannine K. Brown, and Nicholas Perrin, eds., *Dictionary of Jesus and the Gospels*, 2nd ed. (InterVarsity Press, 2013).

Lee I. Levine, *The Ancient Synagogue: The First Thousand Years* (Yale University Press, 2000).

Eric M. Meyers, ed., *Galilee through the Centuries: Confluence of Cultures* (Eisenbrauns, 1999).

Jonathan L. Reed, *Archaeology and the Galilean Jesus: A Re-examination of the Evidence* (Trinity Press, 2000).

E. P. Sanders, *Judaism: Practice and Belief, 63 BCE–66 CE* (Trinity Press, 1992).

James C. Vanderkam, *An Introduction to Early Judaism* (Eerdmans, 2001).

THE JEWISH SCRIPTURES

The Bible that many Christians are familiar with includes sixty-six writings (often called "books") divided into two sections: the Old Testament and the New Testament. Some Christian traditions include other writings, called the Apocrypha, which form a third section between the Old and New Testaments.

The Old Testament writings were originally written in Hebrew (a very few later passages were apparently originally written in Aramaic, a cousin of Hebrew which became the mother tongue of Galilean Jews in Jesus' day). These writings include the laws, stories, songs, poems, and prophecies of the ancient Hebrews, the Israelite kingdoms that grew from those roots, and the early Jews that emerged after those kingdoms collapsed.

The New Testament writings were originally written in the Greek used as the common language across the Roman Empire in the first century (called Koine Greek). They include four stories of Jesus (the Gospels), an account of the earliest church (Acts), letters written by leaders of the early church (the Epistles), and a Jewish-Christian "apocalypse" (Revelation).

In theory, Jews in the time of Jesus considered as Scripture writings that roughly correspond to the Christian Old Testament, though in a different configuration. In the Gospels, the Jewish Scriptures are most often described as "the Law and the Prophets," though sometimes "the Law" is all that's used. Once they are named as "the Law of Moses, the Prophets, and the Psalms" (Luke 24:44). This three-part description eventually became standard among Jews, and led to the name Tanakh for the Jewish Scriptures, using the first letter in Hebrew of each of those parts.

Torah: the Law of Moses, comprising what Christians call Genesis, Exodus, Leviticus, Numbers, and Deuteronomy.

Nevi'im: the Prophets, including the Former Prophets (Joshua, Judges, Samuel, and Kings), the Latter Prophets (Isaiah, Jeremiah, Ezekiel), and the twelve Minor Prophets (Hosea, Joel, Amos, Obadiah, Jonah, Micah, Nahum, Habakkuk, Zephaniah, Haggai, Zechariah, and Malachi).

Ketuvim: the Writings, consisting of the Psalms, Proverbs, Job, Song of Songs, Ruth, Lamentations, Ecclesiastes, Esther, Daniel, Ezra-Nehemiah, and Chronicles.

You may have noted that I said this was what Jews of Jesus' day considered Scripture "in theory." This canon of Jewish Scripture was not formalized until after the time of Jesus. Practically speaking, the Scriptures of rural Galilean Jews were whichever ones they had access to. This would certainly have included the Torah, likely the Psalms, and probably some of the Prophets, including Isaiah. These were likely written in Hebrew, though they may have been Aramaic translations with accompanying interpretation, called *targumim* (singular *targum*).

Other Jewish writings were also read and widely known during the time of Jesus. Some of these are included in the Apocrypha, the additional writings some Christian traditions include in their Bibles between the Old and New Testaments. Jesus would certainly have heard stories of the Maccabean revolt and the Hasmonean kingdom from the books of Maccabees. He could well have been familiar with the story of Judith. He might have heard about the Wisdom of Solomon from a rabbi.[2]

Jews in Jesus' day considered the Torah to be the rock-solid foundation of all Scripture, given by God to Moses on Mount Sinai. The Prophets and Writings were considered supplemental to the Torah, providing explanation of the Law of Moses, describing how people lived it out, expanding on it with wisdom teaching, providing songs for worship according to the Law, prophetically calling God's people back to the Torah, and so on.

Before the time of Jesus, the Jewish people had created structures and practices for teaching the Torah. Many of these centered on the local synagogue, as described in the previous section.

Rabbis, teachers of Torah and wisdom, became common, even developing different schools of thought around their distinctive interpretations of the Torah. Two giants of early rabbinic teaching were Hillel and Shammai. This rabbinic teaching developed even further after the time of Jesus and became quite sophisticated. The teachings of the rabbis, including some from before and during the time of Jesus, were later compiled in the Mishnah and the Talmud.[3]

Most teaching of the Torah in Jesus' day would have been done by priests, scribes, or local synagogue elders. The Pharisees—a loose association of laypeople (non-priests) dedicated to carefully obeying the Torah—had become popular in Jesus' day, and even the great rabbis Hillel and Shammai were Pharisees. If Jesus were taught by a rabbi in a synagogue school, this rabbi could well have been a Pharisee.

As strange as it might seem to many Christians—who have been taught to think of "the Pharisees" as Jesus' opponents and even to use "Pharisee" as a derogatory term—Jesus had more in common with the Pharisees than with any other Jewish group in the first century. In fact, Jesus' teaching often lines up with the teaching of Hillel. Jesus' debates with and criticisms of the Pharisees in the Gospels, therefore, were more like the squabbles of close siblings than the clashes of bitter enemies.

For further reading (see also the recommended books in the previous section):

Roger Beckwith, *The Old Testament Canon of the New Testament Church and Its Background in Early Judaism* (Eerdmans, 1985).

F. F. Bruce, *The Canon of Scripture* (InterVarsity Press, 1988).

Philip Davies, *Scribes and Schools: The Canonization of the Hebrew Scriptures* (Westminster John Knox, 1998).

Craig A. Evans and Emanuel Tov, eds., *Exploring the Origins of the Bible: Canon Formation in Historical, Literary, and Theological Perspective* (Baker, 2008).

Lee Martin McDonald, *The Biblical Canon: Its Origin, Transmission, and Authority* (Hendrickson, 2007).

Jacob Neusner, *Introduction to Rabbinic Literature* (Doubleday, 1994).

Daniel J. Silver, *The Story of Scripture: From Oral Tradition to the Written Word* (Basic Books, 1990).

Brad H. Young, *Meet the Rabbis: Rabbinic Thought and the Teachings of Jesus* (Baker, 2007).

THE GOSPELS

Scholars generally agree that the Gospels are a form of ancient biography (Greek *bios*), akin to the works of the philosopher Plutarch, the historian Suetonius, and others.[4]

These ancient biographies (plural *bioi*) are similar to modern biographies in that they tell the story of a significant historical person. Like modern biographers, ancient biographers relied on sources for the story they created. They used written sources, oral traditions, and, where possible, personal testimony.

Ancient biographers didn't have the advantages of their modern counterparts—video and audio recordings, extensive libraries and archives, or the internet. They worked with the sources they had, which often wasn't much. Because of this, ancient biographers felt freedom to paraphrase or expand or summarize their sources, and even to fill in gaps with their own creations. Greco-Roman education of the day provided opportunities to practice these skills.

Ancient biographers could include fantastical elements like cosmic portents at the subject's birth or death, or miracles performed by the person or because of their presence. Some of these may have been prompted by a historical event (not necessarily a supernatural or miraculous one), but these were seen as signs of the person's significance no matter whether the events happened as described.

Ancient biographers were also unconcerned with an accurate order of events or even necessarily providing what we might today consider basic biographical information. Dates of the subject's birth and death, places the person lived, their childhood experiences, and so on were often ignored by ancient biographers.

In short, an ancient *bios* was a story about a historical person who was deemed to have public significance, written using prior sources but with some freedom to play with those sources, in order to enlighten the reader about the person's significance and encourage the reader to learn from their life and characteristic ideas.

This describes the Gospels well. Understanding the Gospels as ancient biographies suggests, then, that Jesus was a historical person (not a fictional or mythological character) and that the Gospels reflect a variety of sources, however much each of the gospel authors adapted those sources to portray Jesus in a particular way. And this prompts me to read them through two sets of lenses: a critical historical one and a historical-theological one.

One set of lenses is a historical-theological one: I read the Gospels to learn how each of them interpreted the stories and traditions of Jesus they had inherited to understand Jesus for their own time. In general, each gospel account emphasizes different aspects of Jesus. In some ways they highlight those aspects beyond what I imagine Jesus of Nazareth himself would have found comfortable.

Mark highlights Jesus as the "messianic servant" of Isaiah, especially emphasizing Jesus' suffering and death as critical for understanding Jesus' identity as Messiah (promised king in the line of David) and the nature of God's reign.

Matthew builds on Mark, but also highlights Jesus as the "messianic teacher" who authoritatively interprets Torah for his followers in the messianic age.

Luke builds on (and to an extent critiques) Mark and Matthew, but highlights Jesus as "messianic peacemaker" who shows the way of peace and brings about inclusion for the marginalized and justice for the oppressed.

John often (but not entirely) ignores Mark, Matthew, and Luke, and highlights Jesus as "divine messiah" who reveals God to the world and draws the world to God.

The other set of lenses I use in reading the Gospels is a critical historical one: I read through the Gospels (and other ancient Christian and non-Christian writings, as well as archaeological findings) to learn who Jesus was as a person in history. We'll dig into this more in the next section, but let's focus first on the sources the gospel authors used.

Among the key questions that historians ask, two are "What sources did the Gospels use?" and "How reliable were these sources?" Well, we can't answer these questions with certainty, because we don't have access to most of the gospel writers' sources. However, we can say a few things with varying degrees of probability.

The gospel of Mark was a major source for Matthew and Luke. John was probably at least aware of Mark's gospel. (Note that when I refer to "John" being aware of Mark's gospel, or similar statements, I mean "the author of John's gospel" who may or may not have been the traditionally understood author.)

Mark was likely written thirty-five to forty-five years after Jesus (65–75 CE). We can't say with any certainty what Mark's sources might have been, though I'll shortly name some that are likely. Mark's gospel has an oral storytelling style, which suggests it could reflect at least aspects of a common oral story of Jesus.

The gospel of Matthew was possibly a source for Luke, and John may have known *the gospel of Luke*. These possibilities are less sure than that Mark was a major source for Matthew and Luke. Matthew's gospel was likely written forty-five to sixty years after Jesus (75–90 CE), and Luke's gospel fifty-five to seventy years after Jesus (85–100 CE). John's gospel probably dates to the very end of the first century or the early second century CE.

Various threads suggest oral traditions about Jesus that predate Mark's gospel and are used by the Gospels in different ways.

There are some *teachings of Jesus* that cross various early Christian writings and point to the possibility of a loose collection of such teachings passed around orally and circulated widely (it's possible some were written down).

Paul, writing about fifteen to thirty years after Jesus (45–60 CE), shares teachings of Jesus about divorce and remarriage (1 Corinthians 7:10–11), about gospel missionaries receiving compensation for their work (1 Corinthians 9:14), about love of enemy (Romans 12:14–21), and about events at the end of the age (1 Thessalonians 4:13–5:11) that are reflected in the synoptic gospels of Matthew, Mark, and Luke (see, respectively, Mark 10:11–12; Luke 10:7; Matthew 5:44; Luke 6:27–28; Matthew 23–24).

The letter of James, writing possibly as early as thirty years after Jesus (60–80 CE), has much that reflects Jesus' teaching in the synoptic gospels (James 2:5, 8; 4:11–12; 5:1–6, 12), especially what we know of as the Sermon on the Mount or Sermon on the Plain (Matthew 5–7; Luke 6:17–49).

These and other teachings of Jesus are also reflected in other early Christian writings not found in the New Testament, like the Didache (90–110 CE) and the Gospel of Thomas (100–150 CE),[5] as well as in other early gospels known only by manuscript fragments or quotation by later authors.

There is also evidence of a possible early *story of Jesus* that was told orally before Mark was written, possibly even before Paul wrote his letters.

Paul uses technical language that was used to describe the careful communication of oral tradition when he speaks of "receiving" (Greek *paralambanō*) and "passing on" (*paradidōmi*) traditions about Jesus' last supper with his disciples (1 Corinthians 11:23–25) and about Jesus' death, burial, and resurrection (1 Corinthians 15:3–5).

Other possible bits of a "Jesus story" reflected in the New Testament, before any of the Gospels were written or widely known, include Jesus' Jewish lineage (Romans 1:3; 9:4–5; Galatians 4:4), his temptations (Hebrews 4:14–15), his use of "Abba" in referring to God (Romans 8:15–16; Galatians 4:6), his miracle-working (2 Corinthians 12:12), his anguish in Gethsemane (Hebrews 5:7), and his suffering outside the gates of Jerusalem (Hebrews 13:12).

From what we know of Paul's early life as a Jesus follower (see Galatians 1–2), it seems likely that Paul received the traditions he explicitly mentions or alludes to from one of Jesus' first disciples within a few years of Jesus' death. Paul's use of this technical language of formally receiving and passing on tradition in his writings, with ideas about "tradition" learned from his Pharisaic training (Galatians 1:14), suggests that he was concerned about carefully passing along what he had learned about Jesus (Romans 6:17; 1 Corinthians 11:2, 23; 15:3; see also 2 Thessalonians 2:15; 3:6).

There's good reason, therefore, to think that at least some of the sources used by the gospel authors were both very early and had a high degree of reliability. This in turn increases the likelihood that other sources they used were relatively reliable as well. Luke, at the very least, describes his work in researching his gospel in the terms of an ancient historian—using a variety of sources, checking out their reliability—even as he crafts his story of Jesus in the way of an ancient biography (Luke 1:1–4).

What does this mean for whether Jesus actually read the seven scriptural passages I've highlighted in this book, in the way that I've described?

Each of the seven texts I've chosen to focus on has a good likelihood of being used by Jesus in much the way the Gospels describe things. That's partly why I chose them.

There's no reason to doubt Jesus' familiarity with Deuteronomy 6:4–9 or Leviticus 19:18 or that he taught about them in the way the Gospels describe. These were familiar texts in first-century Judaism, and their frequent appearance in the writings of the first-century Christian movement point to a strong memory of Jesus emphasizing these texts (outside the Gospels, Romans 13:8–10; 1 Corinthians 8:4–6; Galatians 5:14; 1 Thessalonians 4:9; James 2:8; 1 Peter 4:8; 1 John 3:11, 23; 4:7–21; Didache 1:1–2).

Likewise, Jesus' prominent use of Isaiah, including using Isaiah as a lens for reading the rest of the Jewish Scriptures, has parallels in other early Jewish groups, most prominently the Essenes (the separationist sect that copied and wrote the Dead

Sea Scrolls). Isaiah also plays a prominent role in the rest of the New Testament, even specifically Isaiah 6 and 61, which could suggest a strong memory of Jesus' use of Isaiah.

Similar realities hold true also for Psalm 110 (the most quoted or echoed Old Testament chapter in the New Testament), Daniel 7:13–14, and Hosea 6:6 (though somewhat less so for this text).

For further reading on the Gospels (those marked with an asterisk are the most accessible for nonspecialists):

Richard Bauckham, *Jesus and the Eyewitnesses: The Gospels as Eyewitness Testimony* (Eerdmans, 2006).

Helen K. Bond, *The First Biography of Jesus: Genre and Meaning in Mark's Gospel* (Eerdmans, 2020).

*Richard A. Burridge, *Four Gospels, One Jesus: A Symbolic Reading*, 3rd ed. (Eerdmans, 2014).

Richard A. Burridge, *What Are the Gospels? A Comparison with Graeco-Roman Biography*, 3rd ed. (Baylor University Press, 2020).

John T. Carroll, *Jesus and the Gospels: An Introduction* (Westminster John Knox, 2016).

Mark Goodacre, *The Synoptic Problem: A Way through the Maze* (T&T Clark, 2001).

Joel B. Green, Jeannine K. Brown, and Nicholas Perrin, eds., *Dictionary of Jesus and the Gospels*, 2nd ed. (InterVarsity Press, 2013).

Amy-Jill Levine, *Short Stories by Jesus: The Enigmatic Parables of a Controversial Rabbi* (HarperOne, 2015).

Jonathan Pennington, *Reading the Gospels Wisely: A Narrative and Theological Introduction* (Baker, 2012).

Graham Stanton, *The Gospels and Jesus*, 2nd ed. (Oxford University Press, 2002).

*Mark L. Strauss, *Four Portraits, One Jesus: A Survey of Jesus and the Gospels*, 2nd ed. (Zondervan, 2020).

JESUS OF NAZARETH

Who was Jesus of Nazareth as a man in history? Who was this first-century Galilean Jew whose name is now known throughout the world? What can we say about Jesus from a historical perspective?

Like any of the topics sketched out here, this would take at least a whole book to dig into (I name several in the list that follows). In summary, though, I think Jesus of Nazareth would have seen himself primarily as a prophet, along the lines of Elijah and Elisha—two ancient, heroic prophets from the same region as Jesus—but with the theological and eschatological vision of Isaiah ("eschatological" refers to beliefs about a future culmination of human history).

This "Jesus as eschatological (or apocalyptic) prophet" idea aligns with the thinking of a wide cross-section of historical Jesus scholars—as close to a consensus as one can get. In particular, and again, roughly in line with this scholarly consensus, I think that the following statements are true:

Jesus was born toward the end of the reign of Herod the Great (around 6–4 BCE). He grew up in Nazareth in Galilee.

Jesus announced that Isaiah's promised "reign of God" was imminent—God's dominion of true justice and lasting peace on earth, bringing flourishing life for God's people and all creation, in contrast to the "kingdoms" of this world.

Jesus gathered disciples and taught them his interpretation of the Torah, focusing moral obligations around loving God preeminently by loving others, including neighbors, strangers, and enemies.

Influenced by Isaiah's "peaceable kingdom" visions, Jesus taught and lived out a form of nonviolent resistance to evil oppressors.

Jesus, like the ancient prophets Elijah and Elisha before him, paid special attention to the poor, widows, children, and others impoverished in power.

Jesus shared meals with those deemed sinners as well as the religiously powerful.

Jesus, following Elijah's and Elisha's footsteps, became known as a healer. (Whether or not these healings were miraculous, Jesus' reputation as a healer is one thing even ancient non-Christian references to Jesus highlight.)

At some point, Jesus began to take on a messianic mantle, presenting himself as Isaiah's "servant" who would bring about God's reign in its fullness. (As noted earlier, "Messiah" does not in itself imply divinity.)

Jesus lived and taught these things in such a way that he was deemed an enemy of powerful people, including the Roman state, and so was crucified. This happened while Pontius Pilate was governor of Judea (between 26–36 CE).

While historians won't touch Jesus' resurrection (it stands outside critical historical investigation), there is ample evidence that several of Jesus' followers—and even some of his doubters—claimed to see Jesus alive after his death. For instance, see 1 Corinthians 15:3–8, where Paul again uses the technical language of receiving an earlier tradition from someone before him.

I not only find the historical Jesus of Nazareth to be a compelling person. I also find the canonical Gospels' *bioi* of Jesus to be compelling interpretations of Jesus' life and teaching and larger significance. And this—along with other factors such as my own spiritual experience—compels me to believe in Jesus as Messiah bringing about God's reign on earth, as Rabbi teaching the ways of God to shape our faith and life, as Lord owning our allegiance above all other powers of this world, as Savior bringing about justice and peace and life for all, and as God incarnate revealing God as God truly is.

For further reading on the historical Jesus, from a variety of perspectives (those marked with an asterisk are the most accessible for nonspecialists):

Dale C. Allison, *Constructing Jesus: Memory, Imagination, and History* (Baker, 2010).

Dale C. Allison, *Jesus of Nazareth: Millenarian Prophet* (Fortress Press, 1998).

*Helen K. Bond, *The Historical Jesus: A Guide for the Perplexed* (T&T Clark, 2012).

Bart D. Ehrman, *Jesus: Apocalyptic Prophet of the New Millennium* (Oxford University Press, 1999).

*Paula Frederiksen, *Jesus of Nazareth, King of the Jews: A Jewish Life and the Emergence of Christianity* (Vintage, 1999).

Anthony Le Donne, *Historical Jesus: What Can We Know and How Can We Know It?* (Eerdmans, 2011).

John P. Meier, *A Marginal Jew: Rethinking the Historical Jesus*, 5 vols. (Doubleday and Yale University Press, 1991–2016).

*E. P. Sanders, *The Historical Figure of Jesus* (Penguin, 1993).

E. P. Sanders, *Jesus and Judaism* (Fortress Press, 1985).

Geza Vermes, *The Religion of Jesus the Jew* (Fortress Press, 1993).

N. T. Wright, *Jesus and the Victory of God* (Fortress Press, 1996).

*N. T. Wright, *Simply Jesus: A New Vision of Who He Was, What He Did, and Why He Matters* (HarperOne, 2011).

Study Guide

THIS BOOK GREW out of a sermon series and a continuing education course, so it lends itself to small group study.
Consider using this book for a book study, and feel free to use
or adapt the following to guide your conversations. Or use this
guide for your own individual reflection and action.

If you are using this for a group book study, you could do this
as a ten-session series or seven-session one. A ten-session series
could cover one of the following sections each session. A seven-session series could focus on the seven core chapters (chs. 1–7),
perhaps bringing one or two questions from "Preparing to Read
the Bible with Jesus" into the first session on chapter 1, and then
bringing one or two questions from "Continuing to Read the
Bible with Jesus" into the last session on chapter 7.

PREPARING TO READ THE BIBLE WITH JESUS
Questions to ponder:
1. What is the problem with claiming that "the Bible is clear"
   (p. 20)? What realities does the author describe to illus-
   trate the problem with this claim? How have you seen this
   "pervasive interpretive pluralism" in your own experience
   of church and Christianity?

2. "The question of how we as Christians should read the Bible isn't as straightforward, or as benign, as we might be tempted to think" (p. 21). What "bad readings" of the Bible have you seen? How have they caused real-life harm to people?

3. "Here's my audacious claim: *Jesus read his Scriptures in a distinctive way, and so we should follow Jesus in the way he read his Scriptures*" (p. 21). Why does the author call this an audacious claim? Before reading the rest of the book, what do you think of this claim?

4. The author describes the Christian life as "following Jesus" (p. 21). What are some potential problems with thinking of the Christian life in this way? What are the advantages of doing so? Is this the way you have thought about your faith and life as a Christian?

Turning thought into action:

1. Look for examples of Christians claiming that "the Bible is clear" while disagreeing about how to read the Bible. Reflect on what might be motivating people to make that claim. Consider how you might respond to Christians you know who make that claim, especially when their reading of the Bible is causing harm to others.

2. As you go through your day, think about what it might mean to follow Jesus in the particular circumstances you encounter and your interactions with people. Strive to live out each day based on your understanding of the values, motivations, teachings, and example of Jesus.

CHAPTER 1: THE SHEMA
Questions to ponder:

1. Do you, or perhaps your parents or grandparents, have a favorite Bible? Perhaps it's one that has important life and family events recorded inside, or handwritten notes in the margins, or bits of paper from church events. Reflect on how that particular book has been important to you or your family.

2. Do you have a story of a time when reading the Bible was especially significant for you? Why was it so significant at that moment?

3. Have you ever considered the fact that "personal Bible reading" is a recent innovation, "a perk of modern Western Christianity" (p. 30)? What thoughts, feelings, or questions about this come to mind for you?

4. The author lists some ways that Jesus would have engaged his Scriptures during daily life growing up in Nazareth (p. 32). How do you engage Scripture in your daily life? What advantages do we have today that make it easier to engage with Scripture regularly? What obstacles do we have today that make this harder?

5. The author sums up the significance of the Shema by saying it is "about undivided devotion to our Creator" (p. 35). What stands out to you from this summary of the Shema and the author's longer description of this?

6. The author lists several ways Christians today show their love for God (p. 36–37). What are they? Can you think of others? Are some of these better than others? Why?

Turning thought into action:

1. Find new ways to engage with Scripture in your daily life. Try listening to the Bible as an audiobook, creating play-lists of songs based on Scripture texts, or pausing through-out the day to ponder a favorite Bible verse.
   Talk with others to discover other ideas, both for your personal life and for your community life within your church.

2. As you go through your day, think about Jesus' greatest commandment, to love God with undivided devotion. Try applying this idea to everything you do, seeking to love God through your work, your learning, your play, your rest, your relationships, your prayer, and more.

CHAPTER 2: THE SHEMA, EXTENDED EDITION
Questions to ponder:

1. What do you think about the idea that there are "heavier" and "lighter" commands or teachings in the Bible, some which are more important or central than others (p. 42)? Is this the way you were taught to think of the Bible? What difference does this make for how you read Scripture?

2. It is a common Jewish understanding to think of the Law of Moses, and in particular the Ten Commandments, as describing "both the 'vertical' (obligations toward God) and the 'horizontal' (obligations toward others)" (p. 43). Have you come across this idea before? How does this help you better understand and appreciate the Law of Moses or the Ten Commandments?

3. "According to Jesus, we love God, first and foremost and always, by loving other people" (p. 44). What do you think of this idea? What are the good things the author lists which are *not* the primary ways we are called to love God? How does thinking of these as "good things" but not "the main thing" help clarify our obligations toward God and others?

4. Consider how the author sums up who our neighbor is according to Jesus (p. 47). How does he describe what "as ourselves" means? Does this convey what you think Jesus is getting at with his teaching? Would you add anything else to these descriptions, or change them in any way?

5. Does your church or denomination have a confession of faith or similar? Does it reference Jesus' twofold love commandment? What difference might it make for our churches and denominations if we included this prominently in our confessions of faith?

6. "If our interpretation of a passage in the Bible leads us to not love another person in the way the foreigner good Samaritan loved that enemy Jew in need—open-handed, with open arms—then we are not reading the Bible rightly" (p. 50). How have you seen interpretations of the Bible that do not lead to loving others in the way of Jesus? How have you seen interpretations of the Bible that do?

Turning thought into action:

1. As you go through your day, consider the neighbors you encounter. Talk with others in your church about the church's neighbors. What do you know about them? What

are their hopes, fears, desires, anxieties, struggles, and successes? Find ways to engage with at least one of your neighbors each day to learn about them and love them in practical ways.

2. Who are your enemies, people who actively oppose you in some way, perhaps even seeking to harm you in some way? Consider how you can love them in practical ways, following in the way of Jesus. Pray for them, for their well-being.

CHAPTER 3: JUBILEE!

Questions to ponder:

1. Read Leviticus 25 on the Sabbath year and the year of Jubilee, and then read Isaiah 61. What stands out to you about the Sabbath year and year of Jubilee? How does Isaiah reinterpret these ideas for his own time?

2. Consider the author's definition of economic justice (p. 60). How is economic justice described in the Old Testament and in Jesus' teaching? What might this economic justice look like in our world today? In your neighborhood?

3. How would you describe social justice? Does your understanding of this fit with the author's description of social justice (p. 62)? How does this connect to the commandment to love your neighbor as yourself?

4. Consider the author's definition of power as it relates to social justice (p. 63). What do you think of this description of power and powerlessness? How might this change the way you think about injustices and inequities you see in the world?

5. How have you seen politics in the negative sense the author describes, as "partisan fights over power for our own self-interest" (p. 64)? How have you seen politics played out in the general sense the author describes, as "how human groups organize themselves and make decisions for the common good"?

6. How does the "politics of Jesus" shape how we should or should not be involved in politics as followers of Jesus (p. 64)? Or more broadly, what is the role of the church in bringing about economic and social justice in the world? What is the role of ordinary citizens? Of wealthy people or corporations? Of government?

Turning thought into action:

1. As you go through your day, pay attention to the injustices or inequities you see around you, in the wider world, in your country, in your region, your city or town, your neighborhood, your church, your family. How is power distributed in these settings? Who has less power than others to shape their circumstances? Who has more? Consider how you might empower the powerless around you, so they can shape their circumstances for the better.

2. Consider how you might use the political means at your disposal—those that fit within Jesus' way of nonviolent neighbor-love—to advocate for and stand in solidarity with those around the world or in your community who are experiencing injustice.

CHAPTER 4: A SECRET MESSAGE
Questions to ponder:

1. What do you think of the idea that Jesus had certain books of the Bible that were his favorite (p. 68)? How might this shape our understanding of what it means to say that "all Scripture is inspired by God" (2 Timothy 3:16)? Which books of the Bible would you consider your favorites, and why?

2. How does Jesus look through the letter of the law to the spirit of the law in Leviticus (p. 68)? What difference might that make in how you read the specific commandments in the Law of Moses?

3. Read through Isaiah 40–66. What themes do you see in these chapters that come up frequently in the New Testament? How do these themes in Isaiah change how you understand those themes in the New Testament?

4. What do you think of the idea that the book of Isaiah was written by at least two people at different times (p. 72)? How might this change how you think about the inspiration of Scripture?

5. According to the author, what do the four soils in Jesus' parable of the sower represent (p. 74–76)? What do you think of this interpretation of the four soils? What do you think of the idea that "Jesus' message is a public proclamation" yet "also a secret message, accessible only to those who are willing to set aside their egos in order to save themselves and others"?

6. What should motivate us to read the Bible with humility (see p. 77)? What does that humility look like in practice?

Turning thought into action:

1. Even though not everyone will respond positively to the good news of God's love, we persist in speaking and living it out. Reflecting on the list of ways we might do this (p. 76–77), consider who in your life needs you to persist in sharing and living out God's good news.

2. As you go through your day, think of ways you might plant the seed of the good news of Jesus, the good news of God's reign of justice and peace and life, in the hearts of people around you. Think also of ways your church can do this among the church's neighbors. This might be through words you speak, but it might also be through the way you love them, the "good works" Jesus says we can do which can cause others to "give glory to [our] Father in heaven" (Matthew 5:16).

CHAPTER 5: MERCY, NOT SACRIFICE
Questions to ponder:

1. Reflect on the description of Jesus as a rabbi and his followers as students or disciples (p. 80). How might this shape the way you think of your relationship with Jesus? How might this shape the way you think about what it means to be a church, a community of disciples?

2. Read Hosea 4–6. What were the sins of Israel which made God angry? What was it that God wanted them to do to atone for their sins? How does Hosea 6:6 fit into this context?

3. Read Matthew 9:1–13. What was Jesus doing which prompted criticism and raised questions for these scribes

and Pharisees? How does Jesus' quotation of Hosea 6:6 fit into this context?

4. Read Matthew 12:1–14. What was Jesus doing which prompted criticism and raised questions for these Pharisees? How does Jesus' quotation of Hosea 6:6 fit into this context?

5. What do you think of the idea that "Jesus' innocent self-sacrifice was an end to all sacrifice: not just animal sacrifice, not just religious offerings, but all the ways in which we sacrifice a life to gain the favor of the gods or to create favorable circumstances for ourselves" (p. 91)? How does this fit with your understanding of why Jesus died on the cross?

Turning thought into action:

1. Reflect on Mary's description of mercy in this chapter's vignette (p. 92–93). What power do you have over other people in your life? Think of specific ways you can show them mercy and empower them.

2. As you go through your day, look for instances where people seem to be doing sacrifice instead of being guided by mercy. Notice those impulses in yourself. Find ways to reverse this trend and instead be led by mercy.

CHAPTER 6: DAVID'S SON OR DAVID'S LORD?
Questions to ponder:

1. Why do you think Psalm 110 was so significant for the earliest Christians? Were you surprised to learn that this is the most quoted or alluded to Old Testament chapter in the New Testament?

2. Note the different understandings of a messiah among Jews in Jesus' day (p. 99–100). What was the popular one which the author identifies? How did Jesus agree with this understanding of the Messiah? How did he challenge this understanding of the Messiah?

3. In what ways do Christians today look to use political power, coercion, or violence to make change in the world, even positive change? What do you think Jesus would say to this? What are some alternatives as followers of Jesus for making positive change in the world?

4. What does the author mean by the spiritual forces that "work in and through individual people and groups" (p. 103)? What are the "fouler things at work in the deep places of our world," which are "our true enemies"? What do you think of this way of understanding "spiritual powers"?

5. According to the author, what does it mean to claim that "Jesus is Lord" (p. 105)? What do you think of this description? How have you heard other Christians describing what it means for Jesus to be Lord?

Turning thought into action:

1. Notice the ways Christians take a triumphalist stance in our culture and society, viewing Christianity as superior to other religions, demanding that "Christian values" be privileged in government, and so on. Consider ways you can take a more Jesus-following approach to culture and society, and follow through on those ways.

2. As you go through your day, pay attention to the spiritual forces at work behind the actions of groups and individuals:

the ways power or prestige changes a person, or the ways groups (families, churches, communities, society) can be driven by fear or anger or greed or envy. Seek to counter these spiritual forces by living out faith, hope, and love in the way of Jesus.

CHAPTER 7: THE COMING SON OF MAN
Questions to ponder:

1. Reflect on the summary of the book so far at the beginning of the chapter (p. 108–9). Would you add anything to this description in terms of what you have learned to this point?

2. Do a search for the phrase "son of man" in an online version of the NRSV Updated Edition. Read through the many times "son of man" is used in the New Testament. What strikes you about this? What questions does this raise for you, including those which may not have been answered in this chapter?

3. "When Jesus calls himself the Son of Man, he is emphasizing his full humanity, his true humanity" (p. 111). Why is this significant? Why would Jesus do this?

4. According to the author, what does it mean that humankind has been made "in God's image" (p. 111)? What do you think of this description? How does this influence how we understand Jesus as the Son of Man?

5. Read Daniel 7. What do you think of this prophetic vision? What is the significance of the "one like a son of man" compared to that which has come before (p. 113)? What does this mean for how we understand Jesus as "the Son of Man"?

Turning thought into action:

1. As you go through your day, be attentive to your own humanness: the way your body feels, the way your body moves, the limits of your embodied existence in space and time, the wonder and beauty and glory of your embodied existence in *this* place at *this* time. Thank God for your humanness.

2. Consider the people you encounter in your day-to-day life, your neighbors. Imagine them as "sons of Adam, daughters of Eve, children of Humanity," in kinship with you, created in God's image. Think of ways this might change the way you treat them, and then seek to make those changes.

CONTINUING TO READ THE BIBLE WITH JESUS
Questions to ponder, and turning thought into action:

1. The author gives several suggestions of how we can "allow Scripture to permeate our lives" (p. 117–18). What are some other ideas you have? Choose at least one of these and commit to making that part of your regular routine, or to making it part of your church's regular practice.

2. Reflect on what the heavier and lighter matters of Scripture are, naming them in a list (p. 118–19). How can you view "the lighter matters through the lens of the weightier" and not allow "the lighter matters of Scripture to take the place of" the heavier? Commit yourself to doing these things, following in the way of Jesus.

3. Consider the summary of what it means to "read the Bible to follow Jesus" (p. 120–21). What are some practical ways you can implement these ideas in your everyday life, or in the life of your church?

DIGGING DEEPER
Questions to ponder, and suggestions for digging still deeper:
Jewish life and community in first-century Galilee

1. If you are unfamiliar with the Infancy Gospel of Thomas and the Gospel of Thomas, take some time to read them online (see note 1 under Digging Deeper on p. 164).

2. The author includes a fantasy-style map, *Lower Galilee in Jesus' Day . . .* (p. 126). Research the way Jesus might have traveled from Nazareth to Jerusalem for a Passover, and draw your own fantasy-style map of that journey.

3. What strikes you about the description of village life in Galilee in Jesus' day (p. 125–26)? What is similar to your own experience of where you grew up? What is different?

4. In Jesus' day, devout Jews showed their religious devotion in several ways (p. 127). New Testament scholar E. P. Sanders has described this as the "common Judaism" of the first century CE, things most Jews would have taken for granted as being what it meant to be Jewish (see Sanders's *Judaism: Practice and Belief* listed at the end of the section). If you were to make a list of practices and beliefs that represent "common Christianity" today, what would you include?

5. What strikes you about the description of synagogue worship in the first century (p. 127–28)? How is this similar to or different from your own experience of communal worship, Christian or otherwise?

6. What strikes you about the description of the economic hardships of rural Galilean Jews in the first century

(p. 129)? How is this similar to or different from the economic hardships many people experience today in your region or around the world?

7. Research Herod's temple in first-century Jerusalem, and draw a map or sketch a drawing or build a model of it.

The Jewish Scriptures

1. If you are unfamiliar with the Apocrypha, take some time to read some of these writings online (see note 2 under Digging Deeper on p. 165). First Maccabees is a good one to read to get some of the historical background to Jesus and the Gospels.

2. What strikes you about the description of early rabbinic teaching and learning (p. 134–35)? Do some research on the Rabbis Hillel and Shammai.

3. If you are unfamiliar with the Mishnah and the Talmud, do some exploring of these rabbinic texts online (see note 3 under Digging Deeper on p. 165).

4. What do you think of the author's statement that Jesus' debates with the Pharisees in the Gospels "were more like the squabbles of close siblings than the clashes of bitter enemies" (p. 135)? How does this understanding of the Pharisees, and Jesus' teaching, change the way you think of the Pharisees in the Gospels?

The Gospels and Jesus of Nazareth

1. If you are unfamiliar with other ancient biographies, like those of Plutarch and Suetonius, check them out online (see note 4 under Digging Deeper on p. 165).

2. What do you think of the description of the distinctive perspectives of each of the four Gospels (p. 137–38)? Use the "For further reading" list at the end of the section to learn more about this.

3. How might you summarize the historical reliability of the Gospels (p. 138–41)? Does it bother you that the Gospels may not have been written by eyewitnesses of Jesus? Note that many ancient persons whom historians study, people more prominent in their day than Jesus was, have as little or less in the way of early sources for their lives. This is not unusual.

4. What do you think of the summary of what we can reasonably say about Jesus historically (p. 143–44)? Do you agree that both the Jesus we discover through historical means and the Gospels' interpretations of Jesus' life are compelling for faith in Jesus?

Notes

Preface
1 I'm not the first Anabaptist-Mennonite to consider this. In recent years, Bryan Moyer Suderman developed a series of Bible studies around this theme. For the first of these, see his "Have You Never Read . . . ? Jesus as Interpreter of Scripture in Mark's Gospel," From Our Churches, March 2013, https://www.commonword.ca/ResourceView/82/15547. Others in the broad Anabaptist stream who touch on this include Scot McKnight, *The Jesus Creed: Loving God, Loving Others* (Paraclete Press, 2004); and Michael Hardin, *The Jesus Driven Life: Reconnecting Humanity with Jesus* (JDL Press, 2013).
2 For instance, Rabbi Danya Ruttenburg (@TheRaDR), "The pronoun for God is God," post on X/Twitter, July 15, 2018, https://twitter.com/TheRaDR/status/1018380721461833729.

Preparing to Read the Bible with Jesus
1 Christian Smith, *The Bible Made Impossible: Why Biblicism Is Not a Truly Evangelical Reading of Scripture* (Brazos, 2012).
2 Hans Denck, "Was geredet sei, das die Schrift sagt," in *Schriften II*: 22 ss, 1526.

Chapter 1
1 Two great options for online Bibles are Bible Gateway and STEP Bible.

Chapter 2
1 Found in the Talmud, *Shabbat* 31a; available online at https://www.sefaria.org/Shabbat.31a.6.
2 Paraphrased from "The Apology of Aristides the Philosopher,"

translated by D. M. Kay, accessed August 31, 2023, http://www
.earlychristianwritings.com/text/aristides-kay.html.

3   *The Book of Common Prayer* (Church Publishing Incorporated,
2007), 352; available online at https://en.wikisource.org/wiki/
Book_of_Common_Prayer_(ECUSA).

4   Scot McKnight, *The Jesus Creed: Loving God, Loving Others* (Paraclete
Press, 2004), 8–9.

Chapter 3

1   For example, at this message at Howard University in 2011: https://
youtu.be/nGqP7S_WO6o?si=cYtwEhpKPrSaMVOM.

Chapter 4

1   Emily Dickinson, "Tell all the truth but tell it slant," in *The Poems of
Emily Dickinson: Reading Edition* (Harvard University Press, 1998);
available online at https://www.poetryfoundation.org/poems/56824/
tell-all-the-truth-but-tell-it-slant-1263.

Chapter 6

1   The description of "spiritual forces" offered here owes a great debt
to the work of Walter Wink. See his "powers trilogy": *Naming the
Powers* (Fortress Press, 1984); *Unmasking the Powers* (Fortress Press,
1986); and *Engaging the Powers* (Fortress Press, 1992). For a succinct,
more accessible summary, see his *The Powers That Be: Theology for a
New Millennium* (Doubleday, 1998). The perspective offered here
also owes a great deal to the thinking of Martin Luther King Jr. in
support of nonviolent resistance during the civil rights movement.
See his *Stride Toward Freedom: The Montgomery Story* (Beacon Press,
2010; originally published 1958). For a succinct summary available
online, see "The King Philosophy—Nonviolence365," The King
Center, last modified March 26, 2024, https://thekingcenter.org/
about-tkc/the-king-philosophy/.

Chapter 7

1   This is C. S. Lewis's frequent description of humans throughout his
Chronicles of Narnia series of children's books.

Digging Deeper

1   These can be found online at Gospels.net: the Infancy Gospel of
Thomas at https://www.gospels.net/infancythomas; the Gospel
of Thomas at https://www.gospels.net/thomas.

2   These and other Apocryphal books are available in some Bible

versions. You can access them online at Bible Gateway (choose the New Revised Standard Version Updated Edition).

3 These and other Jewish texts can be found online at Sefaria, https://www.sefaria.org/texts.

4 Plutarch's *Lives* and Suetonius's *Lives of the Twelve Caesars* can be found online at Project Gutenberg.

5 The Didache can be accessed online at Early Christian Writings, https://www.earlychristianwritings.com/text/didache-roberts.html.

The Author

MICHAEL W. PAHL is executive minister of Mennonite Church Manitoba. He has a PhD in theology (biblical studies) from the University of Birmingham (UK). He has over twenty-five years of experience serving in college and seminary and church ministry settings in Canada, the United Kingdom, and the United States. Michael has authored and edited several books, including *The Beginning and the End: Rereading Genesis's Stories and Revelation's Visions* and *From Resurrection to New Creation: A First Journey in Christian Theology*. He lives in Winnipeg, Manitoba, with his wife Larissa, their two dogs, a cat, and occasionally their adult children.